CHANGES IN SCENERY

THIES SCHRÖDER

CHANGES IN SCENERY

CONTEMPORARY LANDSCAPE ARCHITECTURE IN EUROPE

WITH A FOREWORD BY CHRISTOPHE GIROT

Birkhäuser – Publishers for Architecture
Basel · Berlin · Boston

Translation:
Michael Robinson, London

Cover and layout design:
Muriel Comby and Christoph Kloetzli, Basel

This book is also available in a German language edition (ISBN 3-7643-6428-9)

A CIP catalogue record for this book is available from the Library of Congress,
Washington, D. C., USA

Deutsche Bibliothek Cataloging-in-Publication Data

Changes in scenery: contemporary landscape architecture in Europe / Thies Schröder.
[Transl.: Michael Robinson]. - Basel ; Boston ; Berlin : Birkhäuser, 2001
    Dt. Ausg. u.d.T.: Inszenierte Naturen
    ISBN 3-7643-6171-9

© 2001 Birkhäuser – Publishers for Architecture, P.O.Box 133, CH-4010 Basel, Switzerland
 A member of the BertelsmannSpringer Publishing Group

Printed on acid-free paper produced from chlorine-free pulp. TCF ∞
Printed in Germany
ISBN 3-7643-6171-9

9 8 7 6 5 4 3 2 1

CONTENTS

TOWARDS A LANDSCAPE SOCIETY

Europe has undergone a quiet cultural revolution in landscape architecture over recent decades. Previously a domain confined to each country and almost to each distinct region, landscape was understood as the antithesis of the foreign. It was the local mirror of each society's blend of nature and culture. Outside aristocratic parks and gardens, with their exotic plants and imported styles, there were few examples of cross-cultural exchanges in landscape architecture between different European regions before the Second World War. Even when that changed, it still took several generations for foreign ideas and models to become generally accepted in a given cultural context. For instance, why did the Volkspark movement of the 1920's in Germany never cross the Rhine into France? Why is Leberecht Migge about as unknown in France as J.C.N. Forestier in Germany? I do not believe that this is the product of some mutual indifference between countries, because artistic and architectural circles were actively exchanging ideas between France and Germany during that same period. The truth of the matter is that landscape architecture until recently was nothing other than the mirror of local lore and beliefs in nature. These beliefs were not only part of an ingrained tradition dating back to tribal times, they were also the simple expression of an archaic understanding of the surrounding world. The incredible cultural inertia that prevails within landscape architecture is in fact a significant force which design innovation has to contend with. Creativity in this particular domain is almost always in direct friction with references of the past.

What really has changed in the professional realm of landscape architecture in Europe today is the nature of new ideas concerning contemporary landscape architecture. What is the significance and place of all the innovations that we are witnessing? What influence will these projects have on the living environments of tomorrow? Thies Schröder's book shows us that we are at a very specific moment of change and exchange in the history of European landscape architecture, a moment which precedes an important paradigmatic shift in the understanding and use of the garden. After the eras of polite landscape sociology and landscape ecology, we may be heading now for a new genre of landscape society, a society in which the priority will be less on historical and environmental correctness, and much more on the crude reality of contemporary metropolitan life with its direct impact on nature.

The massive mechanisation of the environment in Europe over the last fifty years, whether urban, industrial or rural, as well as the dramatic upheavals created by traffic and commerce infrastructures, have overwhelmingly transformed each and every piece of territory. Today it is quite often difficult to recognise a difference between landscapes from one country to the next, other than by the language of signage. Entire landscape types have de facto become both international and completely anonymous. The emergence of such trans-regional landscape types has blurred the specific difference that once existed from one place to the next. Within this ambivalent context it is important to define and focus on the specific task of the landscape architect. More than just a designer of nature, he or she has become a builder of some local identity within a realm of fragmented non-entities. But the new identity in question, more often than not, can no longer be tied back to tradition, or to some long lost Arcadian image. Any landscape project concerned with this question must satisfy desires for singularity, originality, and positive difference - needs deeply ingrained in each and every culture. It is, therefore, less traditionalism that matters than the inherent capacity of a society to identify with, and appropriate wholeheartedly a symbolic level within the landscape.

It would be wrong, however, to assert that new recipes for landscape design have become interchangeable from one country to the other. There still remain great linguistic, cultural and political differences between European nations, and these differences affect design innovation and design production directly. I believe that we are in a period where the difference in landscape practice between nations are still quite stunning, and it is precisely the great diversity of approaches that makes things particularly interesting right now. This means that similar problems are, for a variety of reasons, solved differently from one country to the next. The landscape projects in each and every country follow different methods and underline different choices and priorities. We are, therefore, entering a phase of landscape dialogue and exchange between European nations. This dialogue stages strong differences, but it also points at significant generation gaps within each country. Through the increasing flux of exchanges

between European schools in recent decades, there has been an increase in what I would call a "transnational design consensus" between the younger, more open generations of landscape architects.

Why has landscape in today's European context taken on such a key position? Landscape is the product of a rather complex amalgamation of memory and innovation in any given place. There is, generally speaking, a short-sightedness in today's society which has led to general environmental amnesia. The very aesthetic foundation of landscape architecture today can, therefore, no longer rely on historic memory and traditional criterias of beauty. If this postulate is true, what kind of beauty are we seeking to define today? The traditional eulogy of beauty and exception can only work if it refers directly to the world that surrounds us and that we live in. The lack of interest in the banal environment that surrounds us, like the most common and innocuous aspects of everyday landscapes, is a deep mistake. For it is only through the better understanding of such simple banalities that we will come to grips with the meaning of landscape today.

The present crisis of mankind has projected landscape architecture and garden design into the limelight of global awareness, one might even say of human salvation. What does a garden show us today? Is it not in part the degree of understanding and respect that we would like to have for natural rhythms? Is it not also the setting of man in his immediate living environment, offering new interpretations of his modern rituals and needs with respect to nature? Cynics would assert that landscape in general is nothing more than the direct expression of a given economic reality and that environmental disinterest and carelessness are the consistent by-products of human priorities and speed. The Twentieth Century showed us essentially two things: first our absolute capacity for human destruction, and second our absolute ability to foster massive environmental destruction from Antartica to the North Pole. Not only are we able to fight and kill ourselves massively, but we are also capable of destabilising and destroying the very world and climate we live in! Our landscape projects are often symbolic reactions to such contempt of nature and neglect. Therefore, the relevant question for landscape architecture today is probably less about beautifying some ugly corner of town, than it is about the long-term understanding of environments that compensate in part all the outrage that modernity and mechanisation have generated. We live in very narcissistic times and need to remember that our present concern for landscape, as our love of nature, refer first and foremost to the survival of our very own species.

In any event, interest in landscape architecture in Europe has become general and widespread. But when speaking of European landscape architecture, one ought to remain cautious; there is to this day no such thing as a European landscape style. What prevails is a wide heterogeneity of landscape practices and educations. It would be wrong to assert that there exists one specific, interchangeable style of landscape architecture throughout Europe, and such a style, applicable from northern Finland to southern Spain, is probably not something to wish for at present. A more adequate description of the state of affairs may be to say that European landscape architecture exists and is recognisable as such because each European nation has a deeply ingrained tradition. Mentalities are slowly changing, and some schools are moving progressively towards a cross-border standardisation of their programmes and methods. The Internet will also play an influential role in accelerating the merger of different European landscape cultures. But the veritable challenge, in decades to come, is whether or not Europe will ever manage to forge its very own school of landscape thinking and design. I believe it will, and I believe that the great variety of approaches that exist here today is a veritable asset for such an endeavour.

Landscape architecture is also becoming a fundamental subject of contemporary philosophy, because it touches upon the realm of nature within societal space. One could ask why there is, all of a sudden, such an attraction for the garden in our hypermodern societies? The garden has come to symbolise a form of resistance, or at least of reaction, to the anonymous and rather systematic globalization of our landscapes. The garden is the living fragment of an impossible whole, as well as the last refuge of a fleeting identity. This is probably where all the finesse and sensitivity of each and every landscape architect really matters and still makes a difference.

Why has landscape architecture, and more particularly European landscape architecture, become so significant and vital in our time? To answer this question would require an elaborate discourse on the meaning of landscape in a world of speed, displacement, chaos, objects, consumerism and, generally speaking, globalization. The heart of the matter remains in the question of identity, be it local, regional or supra-regional, for landscape identity is the complex product of a given culture in a given place at a given time. It would, therefore, be difficult or even unjustified to assert that there exists a common identity between the great Baroque park of Le Nôtre at Versailles and a local park lost in the suburban ghettos of Vaux-en-Velin at the northern periphery of Lyon. The question of landscape identity is not just an issue of national pride; it coincides greatly with comfort, dwelling conditions and the immediate social and political environment. These are the true and tangible dimensions that define the field where the evolution or rather revolution in European landscape architecture is taking place. For we are slowly turning away from the high-brow tradition of landscape gardening and returning to the original vernacular meaning of landscape: an environment which is the bare expression of living conditions in a mass culture. This specific approach will undoubtedly forge new landscape identities beyond the confines of each land. May this book become one of the first stepping-stones in the long and elaborate path leading towards a stronger landscape society in Europe.

FOREWORD BY CHRISTOPHE GIROT

SCALES OF MODERNISM

Enric Batlle and Joan Roig have taken the ideas of Modernism further forward. Their parks are inspired by Gropius and Mies van der Rohe. Clear forms, colours, plants – carefully tailored – as bodies, defining proportions. Anyone standing in the middle of the circular motorway junction to the east of Barcelona, which Batlle i Roig have made into the six hectare Parc Trinitat, will feel as if a kiss has been planted by Gropius. But then there is a disturbing sculpture: a herd of wild horses as a backdrop in the park, excessively large, but three-dimensional on one side only. A copy and a provocation – as though someone had hung an oil painting of a belling stag in Mies van der Rohe's International Exhibition pavilion in Barcelona.

Why keep building on Modernism today, why cultivate it as a design language? Is the idea to set something against it at the same time, to break through it with a casting of wildness and natural force captured and frozen? Joan Roig stresses that any design programme makes sense. He says that a programme of this kind is needed in architecture. And Roig perceives himself as an architect, and also as an architect of landscape, but not as a landscape artist. As he abhors fashions and the *Zeitgeist*, Joan Roig takes Modernism as his programme. It is an expression of the architect's freedom that he breaks through the design language of Modernism, even if it is by using a sculpture that clearly resists the rigid cubature of his planting. Joan Roig praises Claude Monet's pictures, and indeed the Impressionist painters in general. But he says that Monet in particular shows that landscape is not painted as a copy, but created in the mind. For this reason Roig does not cultivate a style, but builds his idea of landscape.

Roig stresses that he loves built and painted landscape. And yet he maintains: "Unlike architecture, or buildings, landscape itself does not have a programme." Landscape's freedom from anything as specific as a programme allows the architect to take the liberty of making individual transpositions from architecture to landscape. Landscape is the tool to formulate a position. At the same time a scale is always woven into the designed landscape – in terms of space, but above all in terms of time. Even the time needed to grow and take care of a park or garden makes it impossible to subject landscape architecture to fleeting fashion.

1
The Parc Nus de la Trinitat is in north-east Barcelona, Spain, inside a circular motorway junction. The functional lucidity of the modern transport engineering construction is continued in the elements of the open space.

2
The scale of the six hectare park is defined by a framework of trees forming a spatially effective filter between the motorways and the park.

3
The sculpture of a herd of wild horses: deliberately disturbing, to stress the architect's freedom.

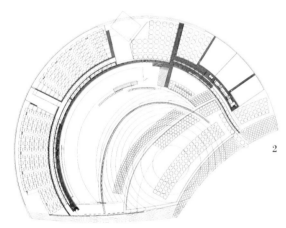

2

3

4

4
The character of Parc Trinitat is based on
clear areas, the juxtaposition of material
textures with vegetation and carefully
placed details like the specially designed
drinking fountains.

5
Entrance area at night.

6
A circular gallery divides the park into an
inner and an outer area. The height differences made it possible to build in facilities for the sports fields in the outer ring
of the park.

5

6

7

8

9

Scale and time are the links with his office partner Enric Batlle, who is so different at first glance. While Roig functions as an architect of landscape, Batlle observes and develops it. He is looking for structures rather than forms, and in doing this makes a distinction between global and individual scales, a scale for the city and a scale for the particular project. Of course all these scales are always in a context, and have to be paid reciprocal attention. But Batlle prefers small scales, and larger projects. He is interested in the idea of a green ring around Barcelona, a matrix of metropolitan ecology, in which the metropolis permits transition to the surrounding areas, without confrontation – and this transition would be designed in sequence. The natural environment and the existing geography are to be respected, but not left in peace.

Batlle is concerned with the identity of the city, which is derived as much from its site between the sea and the mountains as from its new geography, from streets and motorways, industrial concerns and bridges, refuse dumps and cemeteries. "So let us not think of the area around a city as an empty space, and also not as a wood or cultivated fields. Instead of this we strengthen the identity of a region, a city by relating it to geographical features, and making these visible. This is called taming nature, and this is our job. The urban or geographical garden offers new structures to the transformed landscape and uses the integration of complex functions to link these up with the characteristic features of exterior space."

This approach requires creative intervention. For example, the base station in natural stone for the recreational area of Malniu in the Pyrenees supports the existing characteristics of the place. A car-park with service facilities was placed by a lake at the bottom of a mountain path, and offers a sense that it is a pleasant place in which to spend some time. A clear cut-off point is indicated by a usable "wall", which contains the functional areas: thus far with the car, but no further. A creative intervention, but nothing to disturb the mountain landscape, instead an extra element in the local topography.

7

In the Malniu recreation area in the Pyrenees, Spain, the character of the location has been captured by using materials found there.

8

The natural stone walls at the foot of a mountain path are a creative intervention, but they also fit in with the local topography.

9

Walls separate the car-park from the walking area. But the separation is functional in nature and not intended to discriminate culturally: artificial signs are also used beyond the break, to mark the paths.

10

The aim of the open-air system for the town of Sant Cugat del Vallès north-west of Barcelona is to define the topography of a town, its basic forms, by using the landscape itself. A new town is created around an old monastery, and Batlle i Roig's plan mediates between retaining the situation and the sense of space within the landscape and the new requirements of a town. "We were able to meet the requirements of building the town by laying down guidelines that were generally binding for all projects." For this reason plans were drawn up on all scales, from the general layout and context to street furniture. Poplars planted on a grid determine the lines of the paths and streets, and all the open spaces are sown with grass. Simple devices, clear guidelines, a system of open spaces and finally the town as an element of the new landscape.

The Parc de la Riera, which is on a little river, forms the conclusion and transition of the town of Sant Cugat del Vallès to a nature park and to the mountain chain of the Collserola. The park is planted almost completely naturally, and has long, straight paths running through it. The paths pick up the grid of the town's open-space system. Simply constructed bridges in steel and wood lead over the river and are at the same time places that invite visitors to look carefully at the landscape that they are being lifted out of.

10
The Parc de la Riera is part of the open-air system of the town of Sant Cugat del Vallès, Spain. The grid of trees and the network of paths extend from the town into the countryside, and a stretch of river with almost completely natural planting marks the transition.

11
Steel bridges cross the stretch of river in the Parc de la Riera and raise visitors above the landscape.

12
Parc de la Riera, general plan. The existing stretch of river was broadened into pools, to make it flow more slowly and make almost completely natural planting possible.

11

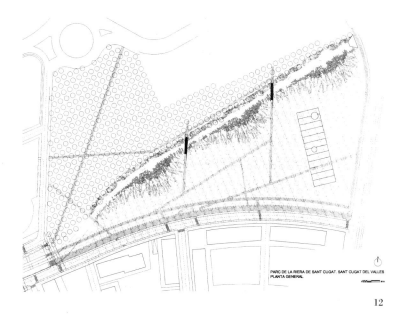

PARC DE LA RIERA DE SANT CUGAT. SANT CUGAT DEL VALLES
PLANTA GENERAL

12

13

14

15

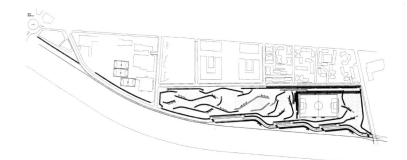

The furniture, light fittings and benches that mark Batlle i Roig's presence in the catalogues of the leading Spanish manufacturer Santa & Coke are constructed as simply as the bridges. Right angles, clear forms and flexibility of use, without historical connotations. "Simplicity" is the key-word for these elements. Metal and wood are used for the plain prototypes that are then slightly modified to fulfil various functions. But the handwriting of the Batlle i Roig office is always clearly visible – the clarity of Modernism.

And so the various scales used by the Batlle i Roig office are placed in a context again. It is only concrete structural and design objects that can become a green ring, a nearby and a faraway circle of landscape identities surrounding Barcelona – as they surround all other cities. Batlle i Roig's aim is to make these characteristics that establish an identity visible and worth seeing as a new geography of the landscape.

13
Parc del Riu Congost in Granollers, Spain. A steel gate as opening and conclusion.

14 | 15
Swivelling steel gates and densely planted strips of vegetation in the Parc del Riu Congost divide the eleven hectare site along the river into manageable units of space.

16
Parc del Riu Congost, general plan.

17

18

19

BATLLE I ROIG, Arquitectes was founded in Barcelona in 1981 by Enric Batlle i Durany and Joan Roig i Duran. Both studied at the Escuela Tècnica Superior de Arquitectura de Barcelona (ETSAB).

Batlle i Roig combine such heterogeneous themes and disciplines as landscape architecture, architecture, urban planning, landscape planning and agricultural planning. They have won numerous prizes, including the Spanish FAD Prize (1985, 1987, 1988, 1994 for the Parc de la Trinitat in Barcelona, 1995 for the Malniu site near Girona, 1996, 1998), the Antonio Camuñas-Award (Madrid, 1990) for the Roques Blanques cemetery, the Andrea Palladio Prize (Vicenza, 1993) for restoring the Palacio Fontes in Murcia, the Bonaplata Prize (Barcelona, 1998) for restoring the public library in an old Torres Amat factory in Sallent, first prize in the competition for the new design for the Barcelona Football Club site (1996), first prize for designing the Montjuïc lakeside in Barcelona (1998) and the first prize in the competition for designing Millennium Building in Eix Macià de Sabadell (1999).

ENRIC BATLLE, born 1956, is an architect and landscape architect. He teaches landscape architecture at the Escuela Tècnica Superior de Arquitectura del Vallès at the Politècnica de Catalunya University.

JOAN ROIG, born 1954, is an architect and professor at the Escuela Tècnica Superior de Arquitectura de Barcelona at the Politècnica de Catalunya University. He was visiting professor at Washington University in Saint Louis, Missouri in 1995.

Enric Batlle and Joan Roig's projects and contributions have been published in many specialist books and magazines. Batlle i Roig have gained international recognition by participating in national and international competitions and by lectures, exhibitions and above all by presenting their work on the Parc Nus de la Trinitat in the exhibition at the International Union of Architects Congress in 1996.

17 | 18
The Parc de l'Estació Vella in Igualada, Spain is on two levels: a promenade at street level and a sequence of higher terraces connected by a system of steps and ramps.

19
The site of the park is former railway land.

20

21

22

20
The upper level of the park forms a town balcony.

21
Concrete slabs and yellow-coloured asphalt are the materials characterizing the park.

22
The rhythmic repetition of furniture and plant tubs along the park promenade picks up the direction of the tracks and the character of the former station.

INVENTING IDEAS

There are several ways of using landscape architecture to define a place. Making a frame, giving a garden a border, creating a setting is only one of the possibilities. A second approach is to stress connections, to place a location in its context, to make the transitions from the whole to its parts stand out. Agence Ter usually takes this second way. Their guiding idea is not to create boundaries, but to open places up. And Agence Ter are increasingly choosing a third way of defining the places affected by their plans. The practice creates images, and these establish an identity for the square, park, courtyard or region they are working on, as a label or brand. The "school garden" for an educational establishment in Nîmes is very effectively made into a brand after defining its function, and then developing meaningful content over and above this. "Aqua Magica" was created for a regional garden show in Bad Oeynhausen and Löhne in Eastern Westphalia, Germany – this was a communication and marketing concept that became a strategy for the open space and regional planning approach.

If you look over Agence Ter's work, you will constantly see how ready they are to link content and image, going well beyond the sensibility and location-specificity of their design. Landscape architecture in an age of brand and market awareness. But a strong label cannot survive without meaningful content. Only good landscape architecture can be really striking.

23   24   25

23 | 24 | 25
Regional Garden Show 2000 Bad Oeyn-
hausen/Löhne, Germany. Water becomes
visible: top of the Water Crater, spraying
umbrellas, gabions following the subter-
ranian salt-water streams.

26

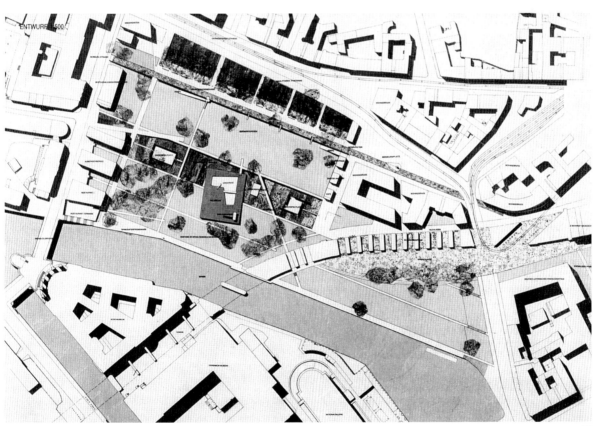

27

26 | 27
*The Monbijoupark site runs parallel
with the bank of the River Spree, and is
laid out in terraces.*

28

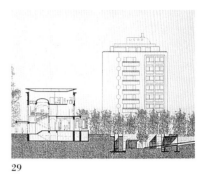

29

"The region takes all" was the reaction to Agence Ter's regional garden show project. It is the quality of the concept as well as the quality of the design that leads to such positive ways of looking at things. The designers achieve this quality by their approach of emphasizing the transitions, the bridges and connections in their sites, in terms of both space and content. And so if "new horizons" are mentioned, this is to be taken both literally and figuratively. One of the landscape architects' attempts to achieve such new horizons was a design for a park – not realized – on the banks of the Seine in Nanterre, France. A roof of trees, which would have reached the height of a recently built motorway viaduct in fifteen years, was to have linked up the views in a new way. Accessible platforms at the level of the crowns of the trees and in the crowns themselves, like forest clearings, would have invited the public to take vertical walks. Agence Ter addresses themes involving experiencing new layers of landscape, its thresholds and transitions.

The name Agence Ter, which suggests Earth Agency, actually relates to the three founders of the firm, Henri Bava, Michel Hoessler and Olivier Philippe. All three see landscape architecture as being about not just designing gardens or squares, but also as affecting the cultural development of a town or region. "Now that there is no longer a clear distinction between the town on the one hand and the landscape that surrounds it on the other, the periphery, the point of transition from town to region, is the area in which we work", says Henri Bava. And so for the Regional Garden Show 2000 the traditional guiding image of a spa region was not just the basis for the design of the exhibition site, but also modified the landscape planning concept for the whole region: it became the land of spas, "Aqua Magica".

28
*Fondation Louis Jeantet, Geneva,
Switzerland: a patio cut into the site gives
access to an underground auditorium.
Its upper edge is both the terrace and the
new base for an old villa.*

29
Section through structures and patio.

One of the things that made Agence Ter link broad themes and tasks in their landscape architecture is that the three founders and directors of the office have double qualifications. Bava and Hoessler both studied first biology and then landscape architecture in Paris, Philippe trained at the French State Academy of Art after studying landscape architecture. This mixture explains the breadth both in terms of content and geography of work that Agence Ter takes on. The practice is based in Paris, but also has a local office in Bad Oeynhausen and one in Kourou, French Guyana, where the landscape architects have realized several designs for squares and open spaces since the early nineties.

Agence Ter's heterogeneous work and designs are linked by their creative style, developed in direct confrontation with artistic attitudes. All the work is presented with effortless ease, including a plan language that is readily accessible.

Of course not everything that Agence Ter devises is realized. Even designs that win first prize are sometimes forgotten; this includes the successful competition entries for the International Garden Show in Dresden and for Monbijou Park in Berlin, both of which would have had considerable impact on these cities, and may still do so eventually. But if a project is accepted and realized, things can move very quickly. "I like playing with time. Working under pressure is more fun." This was Henri Bava's response to the speed at which the regional garden show in Bad Oeynhausen and Löhne had to be realized. Competition won: November 1997. Realization from October 1998. Garden show launch: April 2000. The fact that there was so little time available never suggested to

AGENCE TER

30 | 31
The patio offers intimacy and peace in the middle of the town. When the trees are fully developed they will be the same height as the supporting walls.

AGENCE TER

32
A ramp connects the patio with the street level.

33
Black slate slabs are used for the floor covering in a bed of moss.

34

35

36

Agence Ter that they should produce a modest, especially pragmatic project. On the contrary: the Aqua Magica concept as a message to the region came into being alongside the idea for parks and green areas.

Aqua Magica is an attempt to redefine the notion of a horticultural show. Regional interest in an exhibition of shrubs, copses and tomb planting to show what garden art and landscaping could achieve turned into a project that attracted interest to the region as a whole. Agence Ter did not take a park as its theme, but the element of water, which is staged as a global problem and above all as a regional potential. This frank look from the outside made it possible to use gardens and parks to show what the regional identity of the spa town was based on: the healing salt-water springs. Hot water with a very high salt content rises from geological fault-lines. 150 years ago these healing springs, some of which shoot out of the earth as fountains, became the basis for the development of

34 | 35
Regional Garden Show 2000 Bad Oeyn-
hausen/Löhne: the Water Crater, an
accessible fountain sculpture, is the great
attraction at Aqua Magica. The Miracle
of a Spring, at a depth of 18 metres, is
presented with the sounds of the spheres,
misting effects and mystical light.

36
Water basins show various environments
of water plants: waterlilies in the upper
basin, lotus, pickerelweed and arrowhead
in the lower.

the spas. Now they are becoming the backbone of a new network of town and countryside. The theme: health from water.

This "healing water" is no longer hidden away behind the walls and windows of late 19th century bath-houses or post-Modern Roman baths, but is visible in public space. A new relationship with water is being created – sometimes in parks that are already in existence, like a spa park designed by Peter Joseph Lenné: there is a "park with lakes", a "park with underground springs" and a "salt-water path" as a link between communities. Inquisitive visitors can go eighteen metres down into a well, in a fountain called the "water crater".

Making a regional feature, water, into a key idea and then into a theme for creative invention is typical of the way Agence Ter works. The landscape architects are constantly concerned to make their current concrete task into a big idea. If this is to succeed, they have to relate to the present and to the future, as they anticipate it will be. Two good examples of successful implementation of designs are the open spaces of the villa owned by a foundation in Geneva, Switzerland, and a school site in Nîmes, France. Both projects show the kind of spatial quality that can be achieved if the usual way of laying out a garden either to complement a building or as a secluded and blissful sanctuary is abandoned. Landscape architects and architects have worked together closely and continuously in both Geneva and Nîmes, from design to realization. In each case this led to complete projects in which architecture and landscape architecture blend in with each other.

Two completely different briefs for architects and landscape architects, for converting a villa into the headquarters of a foundation, and for building a new school, were treated very similarly in principle: landscape architecture does not complement architecture, instead they are mutually supportive. The villa in Geneva dates from the early 20th century. It was restored, and at the same time an auditorium was built into the ground floor and basement of a neighbouring building. Agence Ter, working with the Domino group of architects from Geneva, created a new spatial situation making use of the existing sloping site. The point of departure, entrance and circulation centre are now handled in the form of a garden patio of contemporary design, a semi-public space, at the same time intimate because of its sunken site; it leads into the peace of the auditorium. The whole site was highlighted with trees; the courtyard with its paving laid in irregular bands plays with the characteristics of both squares and gardens. In this new ensemble of villa, auditorium, garden patio and large terrace the garden, inside and outside, constantly leads from one set of characteristics to the other.

37

The project in Nîmes is similar, even though the space and the architecture are making quite different statements: a school in a garden, not a school with a garden. The building is split into several wings, structured by the garden. The garden itself plays with the situation of the site. Allowances had to be made for possible flooding of the riverside site. This is why it is structured in peaks and troughs. These height differences create spatial diversity, and the pupils' various cliques make good use of this. The buildings and islands on which time is spent are on the peaks. Bridges and walkways offer paths that lead not just through the garden, but also between the garden and the buildings. Flexible use of a square between the streets and the assembly hall even means that the public is drawn into part of the site at times.

It is this specific concentration on the core of an idea or a design that makes Agence Ter's work understandable. Their strength lies in stressing a single idea that relates design and site place to each other. Variations are permitted only as variants of this key idea, not as contrasts. And yet there is no threat of monotony: for Agence Ter, every garden contains a living world. It has only to be found – or invented.

37
*Lycée Philippe Lamour, Nîmes, France:
a "garden school", which was planned
throughout by architects co-operating
directly with the landscape architects.*

38
*The individual sections of the buildings
can be reached only via concrete bridges.
This gives each unit an intimate and individual quality.*

Henri Bava, born 1957, Michel Hoessler, born 1958 and Olivier
Philippe, born 1954, founded AGENCE TER in Paris in 1986. The
office employs fifteen staff at the time of writing. Agence Ter has
won a number of important competitions since it was founded,
including the competition for a new design for the municipal park
Nordling/Saint-Bernard in Paris in 1992, for the Monbijou Park
in Berlin in 1993, for the garden design for the headquarters of
the Louis Jeantet Foundation in Geneva in 1993, for the International Garden Exhibition in Dresden in 1995, and for the Regional
Garden Show in Bad Oeynhausen/Löhne in 1997. The office has
also won prizes for the outstanding quality of projects realized,
for example the Trophée du Paysage for the Jardin des Acacias in
Nanterre in 1991.

HENRI BAVA taught at the Ecole Nationale Supérieure du Paysage
de Versailles ENSP until 1997. Since then he has been director
of the Institute of Landscape and Gardening at the Universität
Karlsruhe. OLIVIER PHILIPPE teaches at the Ecole Nationale
Supérieure du Paysage de Versailles. MICHEL HOESSLER is director
of the Agence Ter branch in French Guyana.

CONTEMPLATIVE DYNAMICS

Stig L. Andersson – a Danish poet. This thought emerged from the first impressions made by Andersson's work and commentaries. Stig L. Andersson takes in something concrete, and then makes it abstract by putting objects, landscape elements and images into new contexts. The landscape of Denmark, for example, is concrete for him. It is shaped by ice-age moraines. Its character is rolling and rounded. These key features can be transferred to designs, to contexts like farmhouses or playgrounds. But Andersson does not copy the landscape, he searches it – as a concrete entity – to find inspiration through abstraction.

There are twenty-five centimetres of soil on top of the ice-age moraines. It is this layer of cultivated soil that produces new formations, allows plants to grow, offers food. Andersson made this layer of cultured soil into the subject of an exhibition called "Home to the Future" in 1997, by having the exhibition area covered with twenty-five centimetres of rough topsoil. This idea is reminiscent of works by the political concept artist Hans Haacke of New York. "For the exhibition 'Earth Art' at Cornell University (1969), Haacke piled up a biotope about a metre high in a room, and sowed fast-growing grass in it. For his 'Earth Room', 1968, Walter de Maria spread forty-five cubic metres of fresh earth in the rooms of a gallery. All these works […] implant landscape, i.e. external space, in the internal space." (Oswalt: *Implantationen*. In: *Arch+* 142/1998) But Andersson sees cultivated earth differently. Landscape architects are specifically not concerned with the relationship between internal and external space, with an artificial "landscaping of the interior", that "undermines the classical idea of inside and outside", but with the concrete idea that the substrate soil has for the designed landscape. Andersson took the soil out of its context in the exhibition. Soil remained a raw material, there was no design to make it into landscape – or into a work of art.

Andersson explains his landscape design approach by pointing out that he does not formulate concepts or programmes, but instead speaks about a blank sheet of paper that he says acts as a mirror that provokes reflections. The first lines that he puts on paper set a swarm of tiny stories in motion: shapes, moods and pictures that suddenly come together on the paper, as fragments, of course, unclear. "This first act is remembered when the next begins – and the next and the next – experience and knowledge is accumulated."

39   40

But Stig L. Andersson has yet more methods of setting his thoughts in motion. For example, he invented the "Kids' Garden Kit" so that he could see, feel and think like a child himself: three elements, design tools, in a box of sand – seaweed, porphyry, birds' eggs. Associations are triggered, and with them the design process.

Stig L. Andersson has made searching for inspiration his subject. Anyone who thought of Asian gardens when the box of sand with its three elements was mentioned is on the right track. Andersson worked in Tokyo for a few years. He has Asian, and particularly Japanese, inspiration in his bones, and sometimes draws on himself for this. And yet he is not a traditionalist, either in Danish or Japanese terms. He is interested in varying traditions, not in preserving them. "The essence of landscape design lies in permanent change." Variations arise from impressions that form the starting-point of a design when they are condensed into inspirations. "When we are working artistically, knowledge accumulates gradually. Images and ideas are filtered out of the immense range of information available, which is all around us: ancient cultic sites, CNN, advertising, erosion. These are the starting-points we use when we are designing."

39
Nyvej in Glostrup, Denmark: the pavement was considerably widened and given a slate covering in this street redesign, which is part of a renewal concept for the whole inner-city area. Double rows of plane trees will provide a roof for pedestrians in a few years.

40
A sophisticated lighting plan is an essential component of the new design for the town centre. The acrylic columns are warmed by the sun during the day and emit the heat at night in the form of light.

41

42

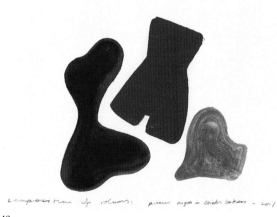

tree forests and two cakes surrounded by trees

setting composed by four volumes, without decided identity

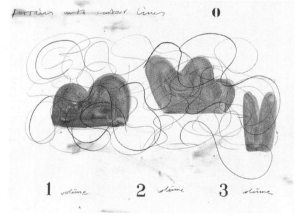

composition of volumes: pinus nigra – whitebeam – soil

terrains with contour lines

0

1 *volume* **2** *volume* **3** *volume*

43

41
Glostrup: Boundary bollards in black Finnish granite.

42
Lamp and bench, detail from the Glostrup municipal park design.

43
"A blank sheet of paper acts as a mirror that provokes reflections. The first lines put on paper set a swarm of tiny stories in motion …"

"Every place represents a new situation", says Andersson. And yet it remains to be seen whether the poetry of his approach derives from himself alone or from the Danish landscape. A pleasant landscape, as Andersson insists.

Stig L. Andersson did not lose touch with Danish garden art even when he was in Asia. The image of Denmark has always been influenced by a concept of *Heimat* that is not anti-modern, but in fact very modern. This is true for both the image the Danes have of themselves, and the way visitors see the country. Therefore, it is only logical for Andersson to emphasize that his point of departure is the concrete textural character of the landscape and its contextual expression – independent of a project's actual site. Perhaps Andersson has again learned to value the fact that Danish garden art, which was Modern in its approach throughout the last century and has always developed in close contact with contemporary art and architecture, has always taken in its direction from dominant styles in Europe, but has at the same time always worked out special features of its own because of its relationship with the Danish countryside, which is shaped by agriculture. Taking account of the context is one of the three most important principles of Andersson's designs, alongside the vocabulary that emerges for each particular location – Andersson also designs outdoor furniture – and the "dynamic planning" which is aimed at changing rather than fixing images. "Landscape design must make it possible to be flexible. Its spatial structure must always be able to absorb change, without the basic idea being lost."

Andersson sees the European landscape as undergoing a climax of shaping and reshaping. "New landscapes are being created, different from those we know from the ice ages. Europe is filled to the brim with such reshaping and with culture, history, tradition and products. New landscapes are emerging today from competition between developing infrastructures and environmental pollution, and climatic and geological processes." This is a development with its own dynamic, and landscape architects can both observe it and intervene in it. "Future generations of landscape architects are faced with an enormous clean-up operation. The take-off-point is primarily the work of the previous generation, characterised by prosperity, industrial efficiency and visions of a future society blessed with light, air and social harmony. The results are raw material pits and dumps that need to be recultivated, polluted soil and waters that need to be cleaned, sealed and deposited, industrial areas that must be built on and housing areas in new suburbs and run-down inner city areas in need of renovation."

44

45

46

44
Residential area design, Ladegårdspar-
ken, Holbæk, Denmark: memories of the
ice age moraine landscape, transplanted
to suburbia.

45
The area of surface ceiling was reduced
by fifty per cent and the site modelled so
that previously essential steps and ramps
were no longer needed.

46
The new design for the open spaces was
made in co-operation with the residents.
Playgrounds and tenants' gardens are
placed on the site like floating islands.

STIG L. ANDERSSON

47
The whole area was planted with various species of cherry at irregular intervals. They are in bloom from late March to early June and mean that the scenery changes constantly.

48

49

50

Andersson sees the periphery as an important working area. He puts in a plea that peripheral spaces "that refer only to themselves, and create their own world" should be linked back into the landscape, the city, the surroundings, and redefined as places. "Such importance was ascribed to the built-up areas of the suburb that they tore themselves free from the realities of everyday life. This is why the connection between everyday life of the inhabitants and the architecture was lost – and architecture lost its balance. It lacks spatial identity, individuality, history and sound principles for building. In past years, public spaces have been artificially revived with the help of trees, with false limbs like art or signs showing the air pollution levels and the temperature. This has been necessary because the sensory systems of the users of public spaces had been greatly reduced due to a lack of challenges and practice. Ultimately design programmes have been implemented to protect users from the traffic and make sure they never have to cope with surprises. But imposing this

48
Urban renewal in Ikast, Denmark: Square by the Music School. "Here visitors can listen to the grey sounds of the square." The design draws its theme from the colours of the moorland that constitutes the site.

49
Polished granite with sunken floodlights. Artificial lighting is very important in this design as well.

50
The design combines some materials that were found in situ, and some re-used and new materials.

51

52

53

reshaping that excludes the landscape and surroundings does not fit in with the way we see nature. Our view of nature involves a clear desire for change, dynamics and surprises, experiences and challenges."

Stig L. Andersson's "dynamic plans" are a positive challenge to change and surprise. The high point so far is his design for a park in the Swedish port of Malmø, which has been brought close to the Danish capital, Copenhagen, by a bridge over the Øresund. Andersson is having biotopes placed at will in the Kanalparken on a former industrial site by the Baltic Sea. The Kanalparken is intended never to seem static, never to be finished. Instead of this, Andersson is looking for a fluent composition made up of varying environments, which visitors experience from walkways and platforms – and which they can change. "It is only parks that are full of life and used by active people

51
Stainless steel edge, marking the transition between the stone dust and the boules green.

52
Granite stone edge, marking the transition between the stone dust and the grass.

53
Cobblestones and a band of rubber carpeting mark the entrance to the Music School.

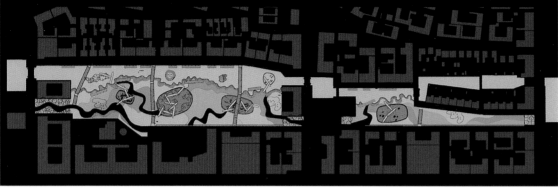

54

that come to life themselves. And then attract even more activity in their turn." Andersson, who also revised the botanical concept for the Tivoli Garden in Copenhagen, has biotope quotations like alder marsh, butterfly meadow, woodland lake or an arm of the sea with jellyfish relocated to Malmø. These can be experienced by touch and sight, and like concrete impressions with abstract ideas about Scandinavian nature. Modern Danish poetry.

STIG L. ANDERSSON, born 1957, is associate professor at the Royal Danish Academy of Art, where he studied architecture. Andersson held a research scholarship in the architecture department of the Institute of Technology in Tokyo from 1986 to 1989, and after that he held a scholarship at the Danish State Art Foundation.

Andersson founded his landscape architecture practice in Copenhagen in 1991. Since then he has won many competitions and acquired numerous commissions in Denmark, Sweden, Japan and Nigeria. His office has five staff at the time of writing.

Stig L. Andersson has taken part in exhibitions in Great Britain, Japan, Spain and Denmark. The most important projects and competition successes are the Kanalparken competition in Malmø,

1999 and the landscape and garden designs for Trekroner School, for the Research Centre in Hørsholm, for Hillerød Cultural Centre and for the Frederikssund Docks (first prize in each case). Realized projects are the designs for the city centres of Glostrup (Nyvej) and Ikast, the Ladegårdsparken on a housing estate in Holbæk and the design for the Bærpark, Danstrup, which is under construction at the time of writing.

54
Kanalparken in Malmø, Sweden: the park is lower than the town, and runs through it like a band of water and fields planted with gramineae. Natural biotope formations are set in the park on islands distributed randomly over the area.

55
Open space with fields of grass. The time factor and the kind of care given to it will determine how the park looks. The design is aimed at dynamic change rather than a finished picture.

56
Alder biotope. Narrow rubber-covered walkways give access to the individual biotopes.

55

56

57

BÜRO KIEFER

DIVERSITY AND REDUCTION

Büro Kiefer raises reduction to the status of principle. The Berlin landscape architects' work is captivatingly simple. Less is more. Büro Kiefer's approach is not minimalist, but reductionist: reducing the design resources in order to grasp necessities. A whole range of ideas is developed by the design team, and alternatives are developed for a specific location, but only the most important, absolutely elemental features survive in the design: intensity through reduction. "What can I take out of my life to make it even more beautiful?"

And so a square remains a square: room to move. A very few structuring elements, and always something to catch the eye and set the scale. If possible something disturbing. Order and chance, absolute severity and complete freedom are mutually dependent. One example of this is the "fish-tanks" in a square outside the new Zentralbahnhof, the central railway station in Berlin directly on the Spree, designed jointly with Martha Schwartz, USA. Enormous aquariums bring life from the river into the station. But they do not dominate the square, which is shimmering with people – even though they set a scale alongside the glass architecture of the new station (design: gmp, Hamburg).

"Coincidentia oppositorum", the interplay of opposites, is what fascinates Kiefer. She derives a contemporary approach to landscape architecture – the intellectual unity of things in their formal difference – from the theories of the 15th century mathematician and philosopher Nicolaus of Cusa, who resisted the dogmatism of medieval faith. There are two design principles: "the continuity of history and the continuity of ideas. Here style is meaningless, it is simply ornament, exchangeable, temporary and transient. Instead of this, the idea is everything."

Designing systematically. A garden responds to the principle of a square. Or of a park, an allotment ensemble, any open space. Reduction is not a question of scale. Gabriele G. Kiefer herself calls this kind of design approach analytical. Central to the process are two principles that run counter to each other, but are fundamentally connected: diversity and reduction. The two "confront each other" until the ideal solution for the place concerned is found. There are three steps in the design process: analysing the place, its spatial ties, its historical dimension. A very small number of concepts act as keys to the work: context, spatial framework, overlapping, separation. They lead to reduction. The application in terms of design: clarity, unambiguity, serial placing, recombination. Free space is created as a counter-world.

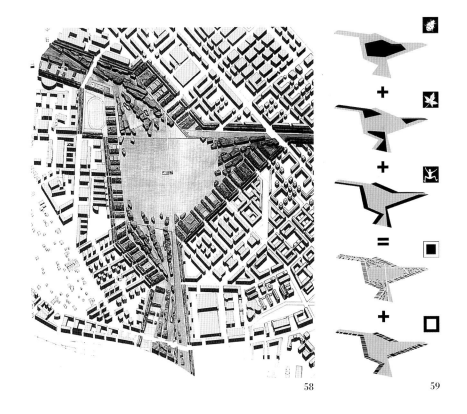

58

59

57
The future park for the Adlershof City of Science and Commerce in Berlin, Germany. A start has been made on building on the site of the future Melli Beese Park.

58
Revised competition concept for the park. The principle of linking with the adjacent parts of the city can be clearly seen.

59
Frame and content. Three types of park become one in terms of space and function: the natural park in the centre, the landscaped park in the joints, the active park in the surrounding chambers.

60   61   62

Büro Kiefer's design principle, a catalogue of criteria linked together as a *formula*, is a universal
one. Their idea of a formula relates back to the same Latin word, which implies 'standard'. The
derivation also goes back to 'forma', 'form', 'shape', of which it is a diminutive. Form and shape
are expressed by Büro Kiefer in a scale, in their own formula. This approach is essentially concrete, as it derives from perceptions of the city. Not by negating their surroundings, but by addressing them, which produces concepts involving new, independent spatial segments and spatial
structures.

Teamwork is a fundamental principle. Hence the office employs a number of different characters,
experiences and interests. Büro Kiefer is an open place, open to international trainees, to architects, to exchanges and contacts. And so it is also a place of learning, where themes, places and
ideas are devised communally. A laboratory for landscape architecture, in which people conduct
experiments, find solutions, reject them again and start looking for new solutions.

60
*Moss is now spreading over the asphalt on
the former airfield.*

61
*Gabion screens with Leipzig porphyry
packing serve as dividing elements in the
park.*

62
*A wooden walkway provides access to the
protected oligotrophic areas in the centre
of the park.*

63

64

65

63
Outside facilities Trumpf Sachsen GmbH,
Neukirch, Germany: water-polished
rolled steel in the form of edge bands,
string-boards and handrails spans the
outside area as a net in which coverings
and items of equipment are suspended.

64 | 65
A game with seriality and layout: strips of
lavender and bush roses, paths covered
with basalt pebbles and slabs. The striped
layout principle meets the firm's requirements.

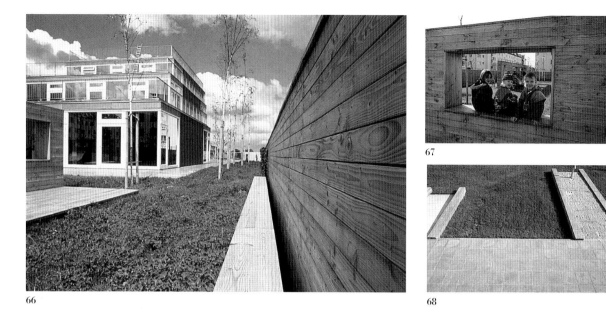

66

67

68

This is how the concept of "park-chambers" was produced for the Melli Beese Park on a former airfield in Adlershof in Berlin. At the time this "City of Science and Commerce" was the most ambitious project in Berlin. Germany's first motorized aircraft took off from Johannisthal/Adlershof airfield in Berlin in the early 20th century. But after two world wars and the division of the city there was no longer any use for the airfield. Air pioneers were followed by vegetation pioneers. The former airfield became a richly varied biotope for urban flora and fauna. This character is retained at the core of the park. Knowledge about history, and demonstrating it visibly, reinforce the identity of the place. "Design that ignores historical associations remains abstract and theoretical and misses the opportunity to discover the poetry of the place." But the park's action areas, the points of transition to the surrounding city, are created in the form of park-chambers. These are delineated by strips of trees and gabions, and provide locations for different uses. These uses are not fixed. Gabriele G. Kiefer is interested above all in the "spatial framework". "I offer a frame, the users offer the content, and that is simply how good parks are created."

66 | 68
K7, a children's day-care centre in the Karow-Nord development area in Weissensee, Berlin: the area outside the centre confronts Karow's colourful diversity with a simple and austere material code.

67
Larch play sculptures.

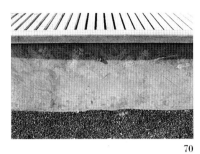

69

70

71

72

69 | 70 | 71 | 72
Goerzallee residential development,
Berlin: classical courtyard elements like
wall and bench are presented in lucid,
reduced forms.

BÜRO KIEFER

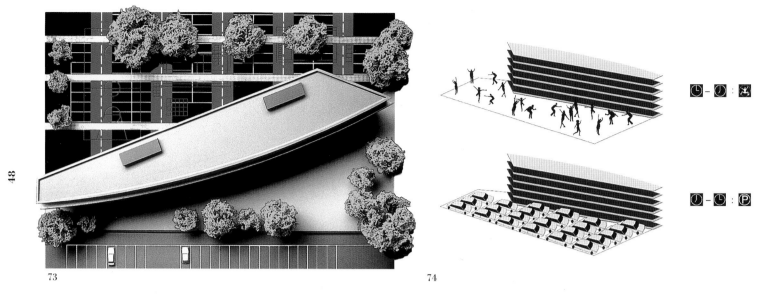

73

74

And yet it is not quite as simple as that. The "framework" has to make the spaces into a coherent whole, as well as dividing them off from each other. It has to emerge as a supporting structure, and not as mere ornament – as a challenge to concept and material. And the spatial framework has to be open to flexible, variable requirements, according to prevailing ideas and the user's wishes. The park concept is defined by the urban development aim, which is to keep the neighbouring districts of Adlershof and Johannisthal together, not to divide them. This works because the park helps the place, in other words the City of Science and Commerce, to find a new identity. The park's theme is to show ruderal plants and high-tech research not as contrasts, but as (civilized) phenomena that relate to each other dialectically. For this reason the ruderal areas of dry grass are treated as inner-urban cultivated landscape. Sheep keep the dry grass stable. People cross these large open spaces, the "counter-world to the compact city" on slightly raised wooden walkways. These walkways are not like the log pathways in a nature conservancy area, but provide lined routes that are appropriate to a high-tech site, though with an element of gentle contrast.

73
Flämingstraße courtyard, Marzahn, Berlin: this low-energy residential building divides the plot into two diagonally. The yard is designed as a combined playground and car-park and is placed on the north side of the building.

74
Divided use according to the time of day in the courtyard.

75
The play-park from the residents' point of view. The design is reduced to two dimensions, complexity emerges on the plane of meaning: colour coding conveys the suggestion of changing use.

BÜRO KIEFER

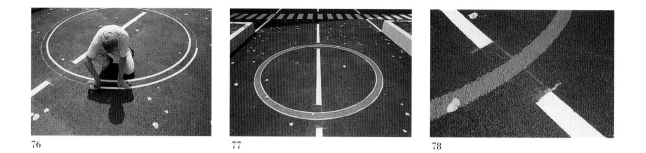

76   77   78

Contrast was also used as a design device in the open spaces around a residential building in the Berlin district of Marzahn. The contrast is not emphasized by addition, but by overlapping the design elements and colours, and also by overlapping functions. Büro Kiefer places an open space at the side of this multi-storey low-energy building (design: Assmann Salomon Scheidt, Berlin), an architectural novelty in the middle of the mass housing estates. On the south side of the building, Büro Kiefer's contribution offers all the conventional design elements of a garden. But on the north side there is a surprising combination of playground and car-park. The two uses are permitted alternately: residents park their cars overnight, and during the day there are games of football, volleyball or shuffleboard.

Overlapping functions in public spaces is a response to the question about the relationship between forms and functions. The design shows a way out of the boredom of spaces with separate functions in the modern city. The overlapping is made possible by a kind of marking that Kiefer calls coding. Here marking, usually used to create order in streets, car-parks or on sports-fields, is developed into a colour concept in its own right. Colours applied over large areas provide a sense of orientation in a residential context that is redefined by the design.

But Kiefer sees an excess of mundane ornament in our everyday lives. So she doesn't use ornament, she creates a sense of direction. It is this experimental passion for rationality that informs all the office's work. But rationality must not be understood as an attitude that is detached from the location and derived only from intellectual disputation. And also not as a rejection of emotion. Colours, plants and materials are reduced, but always used in such a way that emotion is admitted, not excluded. And yet Gabriele G. Kiefer is convinced that her work can ultimately be reduced to a formula. Büro Kiefer constantly works on concretizing and weighting the variables in the formula. In the meantime there is room for experiments, for experimentation as a method for expanding knowledge.

Gabriele G. Kiefer suggests that her practice's success comes from intensive analysis of locations. And here she feels it is more important to work out the analysis and the design as if they were mathematical problems, rather than relying on local knowledge. This self-confidence means that she is able to work with architects. Thus the design for the "Potsdam Biosphere" and the surrounding area, an edutainment venue provided by a German cinema impresario and the town of Potsdam, on the occasion of the Federal Horticultural Show 2001 in Potsdam, was produced in close co-operation with the architects Barkow Leibinger in Berlin. The spatial concept, which borrows from the turbulent shapes of the surrounding area – terminal moraine hills and relics of the military past on the "Bornstedter Feld" conversion area –, largely removes the distinction between inside and outside, landscape and building. This will produce a landscape for learning and experiences that in its new form is somewhere between a Lenné landscape and a virtual entertainment park: flexibility and tradition become guiding principles.

Thus the location acquires a quality that Büro Kiefer sees as a timeless element of open space: being a place that is different. A place for urgency and reflection. A place for encounter and experience. A counter-design to the instrumentalized inner worlds of our society.

79

80

76 | 77 | 78 | 79 | 80
Colour provides structure and orientation.

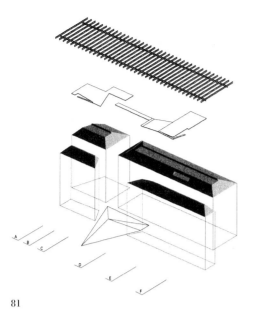

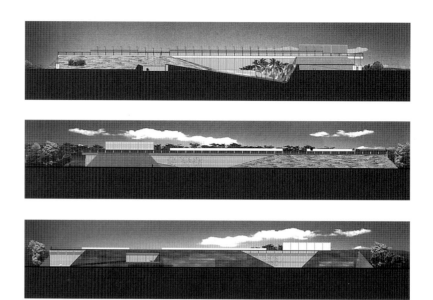

81

82

BÜRO KIEFER was founded in Kreuzberg, Berlin by Gabriele
G. Kiefer in 1990. At the time of writing Büro Kiefer has twenty-
two employees.

GABRIELE G. KIEFER, born 1960, studied landscape architecture at
the Technische Universität Berlin. She worked there as an aca-
demic assistant from 1987 to 1992.
Teaching and lecturing jobs have taken Kiefer to locations including San Francisco, Shenzhen, Milan and Paris. Büro Kiefer's
work has been seen in ventures including Munich, Vienna and
Barcelona.

Büro Kiefer has been successful in competitions and in providing
expert reports for Allermöhe, Hamburg (1993, with architect
Christine Edmaier) and for Six Children's Day-Care Centres in
Berlin (1994, with architects Barkow Leibinger). Büro Kiefer has
won landscape planning report procedures and competitions in
cities including Vienna (exterior installation, 1995) and Berlin
(including the district square in Marzahn, 1996). Realized proj-

ects are the outdoor design for homes in Pestalozzistraße, Berlin
(1990–93), and Goerzallee, Berlin (1993–98), and a Kindergarten
in Karow, Berlin (1994–98). Other important projects are the gar-
den court for a bank in Potsdam (1995), the outdoor design for
a low-energy building in Marzahn, Berlin (1994–98), the gardens
for a residential complex (with architect Klaus Theo Brenner,
Berlin) in Zehlendorf, Berlin (1996–98) and for "Ferropolis –
Stadt aus Eisen" (Iron City) in Sachsen-Anhalt (since 1997).
The Reudnitz district park, Leipzig, a small garden complex in
Potsdam, outdoor facilities for a company headquarters near
Stuttgart, for the Zentralbahnhof in Berlin and for the Potsdam
Biosphere have been under construction since 1999.

81 | 82
*Potsdam Biosphere, Germany: the design
for an edutainment centre links architecture and landscape in a leitmotiv of natural and artificial ramparts.*

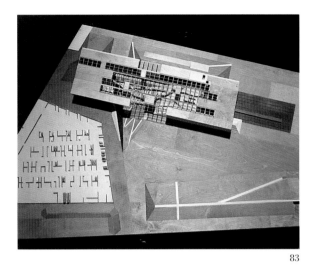

83

84

83
Model of the Potsdam Biosphere and the surrounding area.

84
This design, which breaks down the boundary between landscape and building was produced in close co-operation with the architects Barkow Leibinger, Berlin. Model, sunken garden area.

85

86

ILEX

PERI-URBAIN

"Péri-urbain". This is how the Parc de la Plage Bleue in Valenton is described. The park is south of Paris, and it was here in 1990 that Agence Ilex managed to define a new European prototype for a park on the periphery. An urban park, intended for strolling around and edification, for seeing and being seen, but extending over forty hectares. It is not possible to make this leap in scale without playing with the scale-defining dimensions. Visitors are not offered pergolas or trees to find their way around this park, but the high voltage transmission lines suspended across it. Urbanity is declared to be the image of the periphery, instead of placing periphery and the city centre in a relationship of opposites, and this produces new images of the urban periphery as a park landscape.

In their designs, for example in the refurbishment and remodeling of open spaces in mass housing estates, Martine Rascle and Guerric Péré make the periphery into an intermediate urban space. By doing this, they are opening up a debate about a familiar cultural model: the dualism of centre and periphery. Their thesis: for many people, the periphery is a centre. Hence the idea of removing the programmatic and design distinctions. Why not measure the periphery against the centre (which happens anyway, or certainly has until now, with negative implications of loss of urban quality)? Could we and should we not declare that urban atmosphere, in other words urban quality, is an element of the periphery?

85
A peripheral centre: Agence Ilex success-fully defined a new European park type with the Parc de la Plage Bleue in Valenton, France.

86
High voltage transmission lines set the scale in this park on the site of a former gravel pit.

If this péri-urbanization is to succeed, contemporary developments have to be understood intellectually, as well as in terms of design. Urban life is no longer to be defined as the opposite of rural life, but as a social form that is established over a whole area. "Towns are increasingly becoming part of conurbations in which the boundaries between town and country are increasingly blurred. The edge of one town quite often becomes the edge of the next. A new urban structure emerges, which extends well beyond suburban areas and makes us aware of the lack of traditional urban characteristics. The periphery also suffers from poor legibility, there is a lack of durable images. The dynamics of Modernism can develop here without meeting resistance from historically loaded surroundings." (Gerrit Confurius in *Daidalos* no. 50/1993)

This is the starting-point for many Ilex projects. Increasing the legibility of the periphery means giving shape to it. It is possible to build on existing elements of the technical and transport infrastructure. They can be integrated into the picture as components of the landscape – as Ilex demonstrate with the Parc de la Plage Bleue – instead of being disguised. It would be illusory to present the periphery as a rural counterpart of the city, as an idyll, as both centre and periphery have become different areas within an all-embracing urban culture. For this reason as well Agence Ilex offers garden experience in the form of rented gardens in the middle of a housing estate.

In the nineteen-eighties and nineties, European landscape architects developed the habit of pointing out that the urban periphery had to be treated with the same architectural care as is usually devoted only to the more prestigious city centres. The more "periphery" became synonymous with "problem", with industrial sites going to waste and the social problems of monotonous dormitory towns, the more landscape architecture became concerned with upgrading. Natural stone conquered the squares and courtyards as a paving material, benches and ball-game cages made of stainless steel were considered as vandal-proof as they were elegant. Playground equipment and street furniture became increasingly lavish. But the elegance of these peripheries did not catch on. Residential areas were still just residential areas, but they have rather smart squares now.

Some time and a lot of problematic examples later, it became generally accepted that the point is not just to put a better finish on neglected areas of towns. The landscape architecture had to be appropriate to these places, to their structures and functions. Agence Ilex pursued this approach from the outset, and reshaped the open spaces in several housing estates without any patronizing gestures. They treated each of these spaces as a quite specific site, as an urban site, but not as a

87

88

89

87 | 88 | 89 | 90 | 91 | 92
*The periphery as an urban park. The
periphery is made intelligible by design.*

90

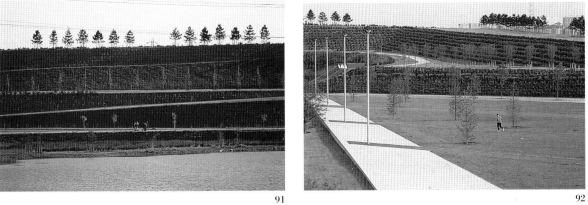

91

92

duplicate of the city centre. This is a crucial difference, as the periphery becomes legible and usable as periphery, in the urban context, but not as simulated centrality for peripheral spaces. Martine Rascle and Guerric Péré define their aim as "giving dignity" to faceless landscapes: by giving them a new face, and not just new make-up. "The landscape of the suburbs is characterized by the normality of mass quality. Massively similar architectural structures, massively similar roads, masses of technical infrastructure. We accept this mass character by designing spaces that are correspondingly sweeping in their dimensions, offering open space as a contrast, not as a rejection of this character. No bucolic hillocks, no intricate fancies, but large-scale designs in dimensions appropriate to the periphery – this produces a new normality for the suburbs."

Of course if such large-scale areas are to be landscaped for recreation and leisure they have to be kept free in the first place. The Département of Val-de-Marne had pursued a forward-looking land use policy. Generous areas to be developed as parks had been kept back in anticipation of demographic and structural changes in the Ile-de-France region around Paris. And when on top of this the public client and the landscape architects themselves are fired by the will to create contemporary landscape architecture, positive examples like the Parc de la Plage Bleue can come into being.

93

93
Jardins familiaux, Bron, Rhône, France: these allotments were reorganized while a housing estate was being expanded. Public pathways were routed so that all the residents could feel part of the gardeners' work and the gardens as the seasons change. The materials and shape used for the little buildings developed by Ilex were

arrived at by plumbing the extremes of the "Swiss chalet" and the "corrugated iron hut".

94
Quartier du Prainet in Décines, France: A raised garden area is intended mainly for children to play in.

95
The estate in the Lyon Banlieue was reconstructed by dividing the traffic routes. This produces a variety of different spatial structures and recreation areas with a sophisticated sense of transition from private to public space.

ILEX

96

97

96
*Lycée de Morestel, Rhône-Alpes, France: a
new school building was sited below a historic castle and at the point of transition
between a cultivated landscape structured
by hedges and wind protection planting.
The plants used, species from the neighbouring meadows, create atmospheric unity
between the park and the open landscape.*

97
*The school complex is tied into the land-
scape context by the use of forms and materials found in situ, like a local limestone.*

"We do some research into the special qualities and positive starting-points a location can offer. It is essential that we approach it with a benevolent eye at this stage. These potentials, which we find in reality, form the basis for imaginative landscape architecture." On the site that later became the Parc de la Plage Bleue, it was the now mythical negative image – exploitation of gravel deposits, neglect, mutilation by infrastructure – that emerged as the prerequisite for a new definition of the place, for its revival. The bad image released a great deal of energy, and so a completely fresh start could be made here.

The open-space concepts for the Quartier du Prainet in Décines and the Quartier des Etats-Unis, both near Lyon, were very different. In the case of the Quartier du Prainet the main thing was to reorganize the pattern of urban access and to develop a decentralized access for all forms of transport instead of a single ring-road concentrating on cars. For the Quartier des États-Unis, which was designed by Tony Garnier and thus associated with his model of an ideal city, the Cité Industrielle, "the originality of the initial concept of a clear sequence of public and private spaces" had to be recreated.

It becomes clear that the potential of a location is not always visible at first sight, it can also derive from a place's surroundings, its history or its problems. A particular quality of light can be a potential of this kind, just as much as a new sense of scale, a material, a specific kind of vegetation.

98
The exterior design for the headquarters of Société Würth in Alsace, France mediates between the infrastructural requirements of an industrial estate and the rural landscape. A framework of trees takes the scale of the landscape right up to the building and at the same time provides a setting for it.

99
The site is divided into three sections: a car-park, an intensively designed garden by the building and open parkland as a transition to the landscape with a view of the Vosges. Once again the trees make the three areas into a whole.

But once one has grasped the potential, then it can be built upon in the design. "We can tie our design into the potential we discover, or we can design a clear contrast, a break with what we have found in situ. In both cases it is essential to have understood the location very well: its components, its possibilities. Only then can we design spaces in such a way that they are appropriate to the location and usable at the same time. For this to be the case, the newly designed places need spatial depth above all, they need to be effective in every dimension, rather than merely a set of decorative accoutrements."

Agence Ilex's landscape architecture is not concerned to offer ubiquitous images, but appropriate responses to particular situations. "For us this means looking not just for an up-to-date form of aesthetic expression, but also an up-to-date strategic approach to a task. Hence our projects are stations, step-by-step aims for permanent changes to the underlying locations and spaces."

100
Quartier des Etats-Unis, Lyon, France:
this ensemble was built as an "ideal city"
in the thirties and was redesigned with an
eye on the original concept as a hierarchi-
cal spatial sequence from the public street
to the private area inside the blocks.

101

Martine Rascle, born 1950, and Guerric Péré, born 1956, founded the AGENCE ILEX landscape architecture practice with Denis Fontaine in Lyon in 1987.

MARTINE RASCLE studied economics in Lyon and landscape architecture at the Ecole Nationale Supérieure du Paysage ENSP in Versailles. GUERRIC PÉRÉ studied geography in Lyon and landscape architecture at the Ecole Nationale Supérieure du Paysage in Versailles.

Major projects and competition successes: Agence Ilex won the Trophée du Paysage prize for the first phase of the Parc de la Plage Bleue, Valenton, which was realized from 1990 to 1996, in 1993. They produced innovative designs for urban open spaces for the Quartier du Prainet in Décines near Lyon (1992–95) and

the Quartier des Etats-Units, Lyon (1994–99), and for the Place Jean-Jaurès, Saint-Etienne in 1997/98 and the Place Valmy, Lyon in 1996–97. The most important gardens and parks – alongside the Parc de la Plage Bleue – are the Jardins Familiaux, Bron, 1993–95, the park for the Würth company, Erstein in 1996–97, Les Berges de L'Ill, Strasbourg, 1996–2000, the garden of the Lycée de Morestel, Morestel in 1993-95 and several parks for Hewlett Packard in L'Isle d'Abeau, Eybens, Ecully and Barcelona. At present the office is working on large-scale projects like the Parc des Oiseaux, Villars-les-Dombes, Bron city centre, ZAC Fenilly technology park, Saint-Priest (all for 2001) and a new design for the Parc des Coudrays, Elancourt (for 2002).
Ilex won the Trophée de l'Arbre d'Or for the Würth park in 2000.

101
One of the courtyard interiors, the
"Chambres vertes", at night.

102

103

LATZ + PARTNER

CONSTRUCTING PHYSICAL NATURE

Latz + Partner work on constructing physical nature. In their joint office, Peter and Anneliese Latz are entrusted with designs for open spatial structures that can be used for a number of purposes. They see landscape architecture as being about dealing with something that is already there, something that offers a basis for new constructions of and with nature.

Constructing nature means experimenting for Latz + Partner. Their commissions are urban development as well as landscape projects, designs for parks, gardens and waste land, and sometimes they are experimental buildings, optimized in terms of ecology and energy. Latz cultivate ecological building and living by the use of highly inventive techniques.

In the seventies, Peter Latz – who came from a large-scale landscape planning background – turned to solving problems on a scale of 1:1. Buildings, landscape and gardens were subjected to experiments under real conditions. Even after he was appointed Professor of Landscape Architecture and Planning at the Technische Universität in Munich-Weihenstephan in 1983, Latz remained curious, and committed to his aim of exploring and testing new technologies for open space and architecture. Influencing the micro-climate, water and recycling cycles and the transitional

102 | 103
Rose garden in Ampertshausen, Bavaria,
Germany: " Pictures are created in
the mind of the beholder, and if they are
Romantic pictures, that is all right!"

104

105

106

zones between inside and outside, so-called "intermediate temperature zones", are fields for exper-imentation and research. The Latz house in Ampertshausen, Bavaria, near the college and yet right out in the country in a hamlet with fifty inhabitants, is a perfect example of a low-energy building.

The Latz garden is also a sample of their own work. The broken-brick walls and above all the box and rose planting show what landscape architecture means to Latz: meticulous attention to detail, to reinforce the individual element as a symbol of the overall concept. Peter Latz and his colleagues work on the practice's building sites themselves: pruning trees, laying paths and walls, planting. And above all in tending the developing project. "The actual potential of a landscape, of a garden, is not seen until the plans are realized and the project is being constructed. And the finishing pro-cess that we carry out on the spot is never over. This is particularly true when planting is under-taken as intensively as we do. A great deal of time needs to be spent on an area before it becomes an attractive park. Unfortunately this level of care is only seldom possible. But if long-term commit-ment can be achieved, as in the case of the landscape park in Duisburg-Nord and the Luxembourg European City project, Kirchberg Plateau, then the quality of what develops is very much higher."

104
The Latz home and office in Amperts-hausen is a perfect example of a low-energy building. The orthogonal pool has a biological-structural function and also links up with the surroundings.

105
First experimental building in Kassel, Germany. An old building was converted into an ecological low-energy house.

106
The campus of the Institute of Land Cultivation and Botany at the Technical University Weihenstephan, Germany, is used as a field for research and experi-mentation.

Latz + Partner refuse to put planning and execution in different hands. "This usually leads to the project's becoming intensely banal. We like to look at what we have devised as it is being implemented, and to make changes on the spot. For this reason we do not give clients a general plan. Ideal plans function as badly as ideal cities. We ask ourselves what concrete resources and possibilities are available for working on a space. Important impetus comes from urban redevelopment. We learned in the seventies not only to plan things but to tackle them, to put them into practice. We have derived our own working method from this, rather than an ideology. And so we hope to acquire clients who will trust what we are doing on the spot."

And it is easy to come to trust Latz + Partner's work when you look at completed projects. In fact their projects always continue to develop ideas and elements from earlier work. Thus the theme of large trees is addressed in the Duisburg-Nord landscape park and – in a different form – in the European City in Kirchberg, Luxembourg. The big trees are just as much a design element in the park on the Bornstedter Feld, which will be opened for the Federal Horticultural Show 2001 in Potsdam, as they are for the park at a Shell research centre in Thornton, Great Britain.

For his project for the Saarbrücken harbour island, Peter Latz developed landscape architecture in the form of dealing with what is found to be present and then perfected the method in Duisburg-Nord. And the idea of opening up the canalized water-curses, developed further in Duisburg-Nord and in the Ulm University gardens and in Thornton to form a water-system in its own right, also recurs in the courtyard of a residential and office project in Munich. Latz + Partner cultivate their handwriting with the "learning progress method" without seeming monotonous in the partial repetition of themes.

Latz + Partner certainly work with what they find, but always within their repertoire. Each park should be in a position to develop gradually. Laying out landscapes and gardens is defined as a cultural task: formerly a means of ensuring survival and then – with increased complexity – garden art. It was only under Modernism that the basis was laid for our present landscapes: industrialized building, landscape management.

Peter Latz teaches landscape architecture as professor at the Technical University in Munich-Weihenstephan. His theme is Modernism there too. "All the professions, landscape architecture, urban development, architecture, go back to the same Modern fundamentals." But he thinks that

107
European City of Luxembourg, Plateau de Kirchberg. A city motorway is being converted into the Avenue J. F. Kennedy, with avenues of trees and generous pedestrian areas.

108

108
A sculptural pond system serves to retain surface water.

110

109
*Existing large trees are replanted
and form a new grove near the planned
European School.*

110
*Excavated material from the road-build-
ing project forms a "dune park" as an
earth sculpture that lends shape to the
space.*

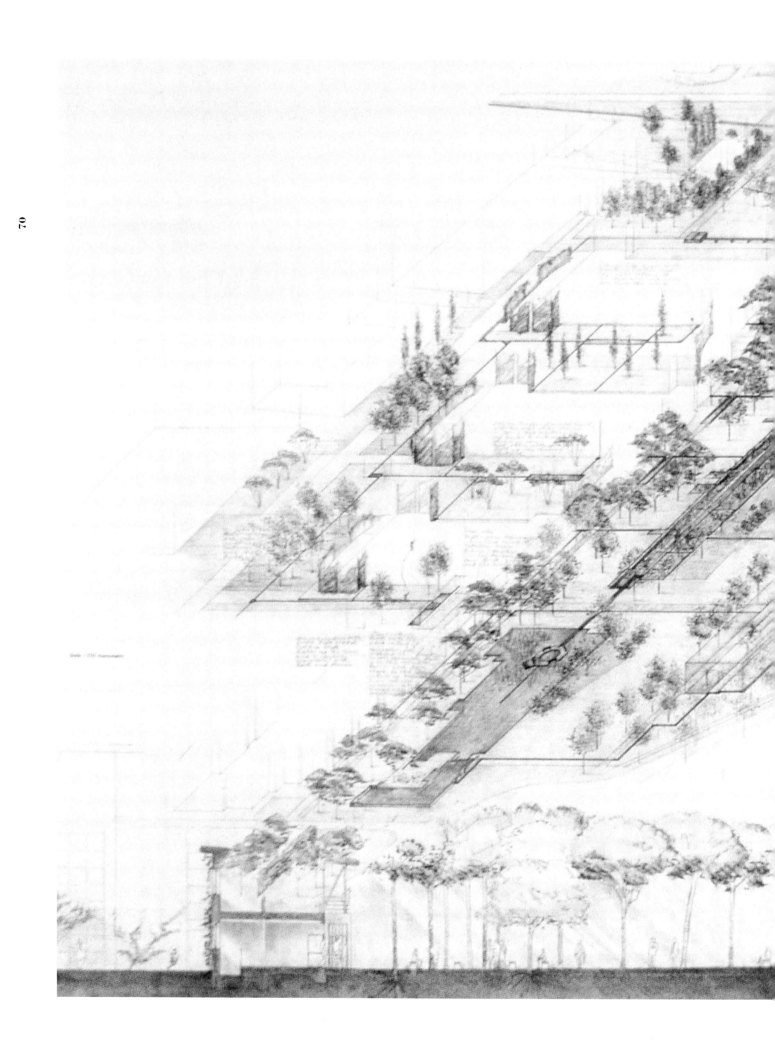

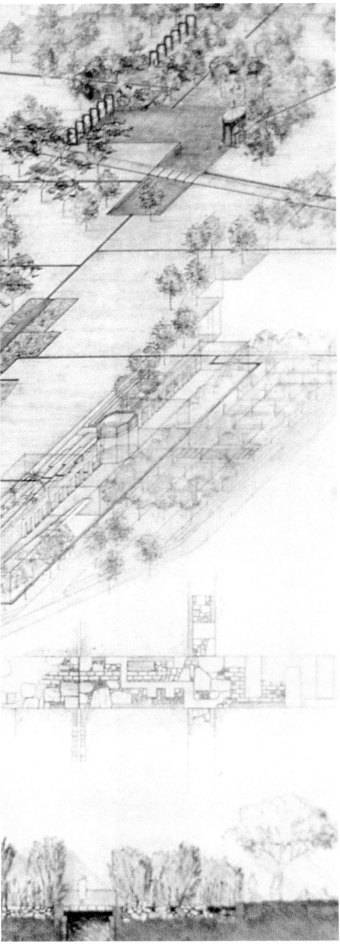

111

Shell Research Centre, Thornton,
Great Britain: structures from existing
buildings become a "New Landscape".
The design was produced in cooperation
with Ian Hamilton Finlay and Pia Simig.

112   113

architecture is distinct from landscape architecture in that its progress was in existence and mani-
fested itself earlier: "Perhaps innovations are not thought of earlier in architecture, but they are
implemented earlier, and thus become visible." Latz detects a time-lag in landscape architecture
vis-à-vis architecture of about ten years. He says this delay is partly because a garden develops
more slowly, but partly because many landscape architects are so naïve. "Taken all in all, landscape architecture is lacking in quality."

And it is also for this reason that Latz works in the fields of urban development, architecture and
landscape architecture. He regrets the fact that the disciplines have been separated in Germany.
In fact he started his office as an urban development practice in the seventies. But Peter Latz did
not become a landscape architect just by chance. He earned money by cultivating fruit and then –
because the profits came in more quickly – with strawberries, while he was still a youth. So he
started to be interested in plants at an early stage. But he did not start to concentrate on landscape
architecture until he was appointed to the chair of landscape architecture at the Gesamthochschule
in Kassel. "But this is true only for our work in Germany. In all other regions, from London via
Luxembourg to Milan we work on urban planning as well."

112 | 113
Regional Central Bank in Kassel: the
main entrance area with evergreen
hedges forms at the same time a public
municipal garden.

Munich airport is close to both office and college – his bags are always packed. Symposia, lectures and seminars all over the world, and also teaching commitments not just at Weihenstephan but also as visiting professor at the University of Pennsylvania, are coordinated from his home and office in Bavaria. This wooden house is an introverted structure. In the centre is an enclosed courtyard, a place where employees can take their break. Greened façades screen off the outside world. A square pool of water forms a link with the open countryside, helped by almost natural planting – and has a function as part of the building's biology as well. Latz is happy to accept the fact that this pool, as a visual feature fronting agricultural landscape, triggers Romantic associations. "I do not design pictures, not even Romantic ones, but spaces for communication. The syntactic level is central to this. Pictures are created in the mind of the beholder, and if they are Romantic pictures, that is all right!" Latz explains the Romantic intentions that are ascribed to him – he has been called an "advocate of ruins", and also a "poet of pollution" – as a biased interpretation of his design method, which always goes back to what is there, in order to develop existing perspectives further.

Peter and Anneliese Latz create timeless structures from a very few elements. These elements are plants as ruderal vegetation, as rose or box-tree beds or as greenery on a façade, trees, and elements that are found on the spot. Thus the structure for the 230 hectare landscape park in Duisburg-Nord is provided by former railway lines: the 'track harp'. Three blast furnaces formerly used for steel production remain in the landscape park, along with the coal bunkers. The bunkers contain gardens and leisure facilities ranging from an exciting slide to climbing walls. One of the

114

115

114
Central office building for DeTeMobil, Bonn, Germany. One of twelve inner courtyards on flat roofs.

115
The façade planting is part of the energy concept for the building.

116

blast furnaces can be visited, and provides an outstanding view of the Ruhr as well as some industrial history. And the material used for the Piazza Metallica between the blast furnaces is a reminder of the place's former function: refining steel. The park as a whole is a convincing reminiscence of the modern industrial era.

Waste land is available all over the world as a new type of open space. But structure, new landscapes, will not be developed on the basis of these areas of waste land until continuous work is put in on constructing nature, with curiosity and delight taken in experiment, to make new natural pictures possible. Latz himself uses a broad range of approaches when looking for such constructions. Elements for his designs are chosen rationally, subjected to precise physical calculations if necessary and sometimes even – as in the case of an ensemble of buildings and hedges – tested in a wind tunnel. But on the other hand, Latz first wrote stories as an approach to the derelict industrial land in Duisburg, stories which then became the basis of the design. Both approaches are brought together by the dominance of culture in the face of nature, even though many people see other images in Latz's parks and gardens.

117

118

119

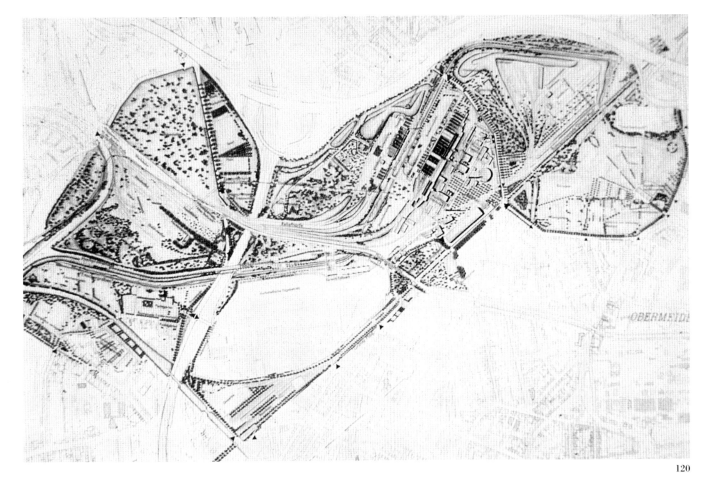

120

116
*Culture before nature: a park that plays
with classical garden images, made mainly of recycled materials, has been created
on the harbour island in Saarbrücken,
Germany, the site of a coal harbour that
has lain unused for decades.*

117 | 118 | 119
*Science City Ulm, Germany: a rainwater
system was built into the open space
design for the new engineering faculty
building.*

120
*The design of the 230 hectare landscape
park in Duisburg-Nord in the Ruhr
district, Germany, is based on a reinter-
pretation of the network of industrial
structures.*

121

122

123

121
The material of the Piazza Metallica
reminds us of the place's former function:
refining steel.

122
New images of nature at former industrial
sites.

123
The park is made up of four overlapping
park concepts including the water-park,
which uses an existing system of canals,
treatment pools and reservoirs. Diving
courses are available.

124   125   126

PETER LATZ, born 1939, and ANNELIESE LATZ work and live in Ampertshausen near Freising in the Munich region. Peter Latz studied landscape architecture at the Technische Universität München-Weihenstephan and urban design at the RWTH Aachen. Anneliese Latz studied landscape architecture at the Technische Universität München-Weihenstephan.

The couple set up their urban, landscape and system planning practice in 1968, with offices in Aachen, Saarbrücken and from 1973 in Kassel, as Peter Latz, who previously taught at the Academies of Architecture in Maastricht and Amsterdam, was appointed Professor of Landscape Architecture at the Gesamt-hochschule in Kassel. In 1983 Latz became Professor of Land-scape Architecture and Planning at the TU München-Weihen-stephan. The Latz + Partner office with twelve landscape archi-tects has been in existence near Munich since 1988. There is still a practice partnership in Kassel (Latz-Riehl practice).

The most important projects and competition successes are the Duisburg-Nord landscape park (1st prize in the international competition as part of the Emscher Park International Building Exhibition), 1991–2000, which was awarded the "First Rosa Barba European Landscape Prize" in Barcelona, 2000; the Volkspark and Federal Horticultural Show Potsdam 2001 (1st prize in the international competition with Jourda and HHS architects), masterplan 1997, subsequent further planning and realization in the southern section of the park; Saarbrücken har-bour island, 1980–89, BDLA award 1989. Latz + Partner designed a park for the Shell Research Centre in Thornton with Ian Hamil-ton Finlay and Pia Simig, Little Sparta, Scotland, first phase realized in 1998/99. They won the competition for the Science City on the Eselsberg for the University of Ulm in 1988 (with Otto Steidle), completed in 1995. Solar City Regensburg was developed in 1995–98 with Thomas Herzog and Norman Foster. The master-plan for the renewal of the European City of Luxembourg, Pla-teau de Kirchberg, for urban design, landscape and art dates from 1990–93, with Caspar König, Jochem Jourdan and Christian Bauer; since then central park areas have been realized and the city motorway converted into a boulevard. The pedestrian area in the town of Melsungen (1st prize in the 1995 competition with HHS Architekten) was redesigned in 1996. Latz + Partner with Manfred Hegger and Peter Lieser submitted development plans for the Frankfurt am Main green belt in 1990.

Building plans for projects including the Wacker-Chemie building in Munich (1st prize in the competition, with Otto Steidle) in 1991–97. The Latz home and office building in Kranzberg, com-pleted in 1992, along with the "Green Buildings", Berlin 1985, and the Latz Passive Solar House in Kassel, 1980–83 are examples of ecological building from the Latz + Partner office.

LATZ + PARTNER

124
A number of small gardens were created in the former ore and coal bunkers.

125
Picking up on the past: starting-point for cultivating discontinuities.

126
The wind wheel is the "engine" for water circulation and part of the overall water system.

PUT NOT YOUR TRUST IN NAÏVE GARDENS!

"Landscape architects usually have a marginal part to play." Michel Desvigne likes to make this his opening remark. The Frenchman, who prefers to do his experimental work on a small scale, and his office partner Christine Dalnoky want to change this. They may not want to change landscape architecture as a whole, but Desvigne & Dalnoky do want at least to have some influence on design developments in the environment – and they want to do this with new creative ideas and approaches on a large scale. A conflict of aims?

This has been the assumption for the last thirty years. For this reason, the handling of landscape started to be professionalized by a process of specialist differentiation. Protecting the landscape was seen as a counterpart to designing it, cultivation was separated from garden design and from environmental management, and landscape architecture was temporarily forced to take a back seat to social and ecological goals. The assumed opposites were dogmatically defended in order to take up a position, instead of sharpening outlines within a process of looking for consensus. Desvigne and Dalnoky want to make artistic and joyful use at least of the marginal influence of landscape architecture on changes in the landscape – their landscape architecture functions as a catalyst, indicator and seed for new developments.

127

128

127
Rue de Meaux, Paris, France: court-yard for a residential building designed by Renzo Piano.

128
"We believe that a garden does not have a spirit until a piece of landscape crystal-lizes within it, along with all necessary rigour."

129
Little money was available for the design. The bolted birches are rejects from a tree nursery, set in square beds with hon-eysuckle as ground-cover.

MICHEL DESVIGNE / CHRISTINE DALNOKY

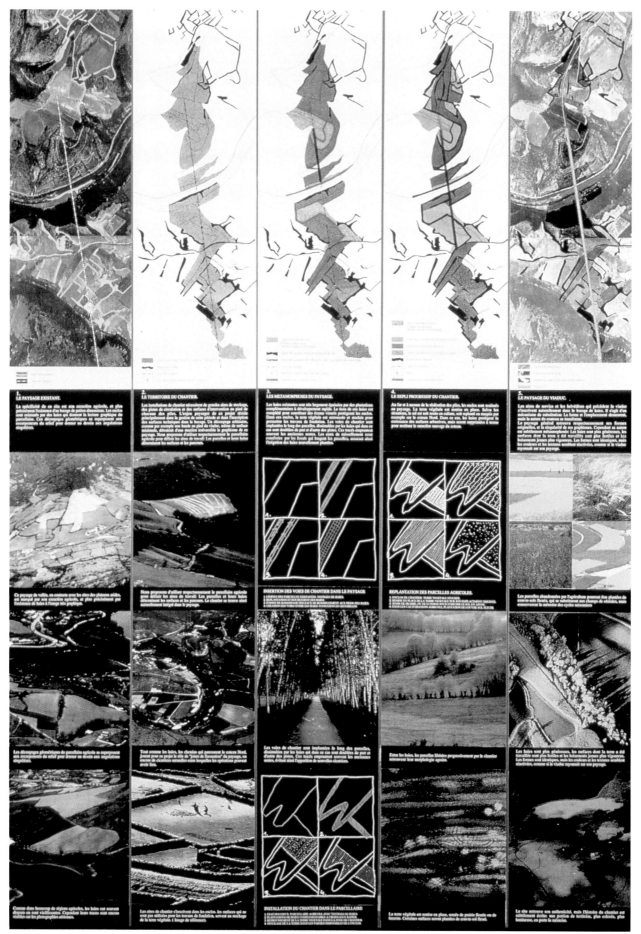

Desvigne and Dalnoky's work as landscape architects is scarcely open to classification, the spectrum being as broad as it possibly could be. It includes studies for the routes and stations of the French TGV express trains, and also the birch grove in a little inner courtyard in the Rue de Meaux in Paris. This landscape garden in the middle of a residential development, designed in 1989 and completed by 1992, is to some extent the point at which Desvigne and Dalnoky's working planes intersect, indicating not an intermediate scale, but probably an intellectual and aesthetic connection of gardens and landscapes. By contrast, the classification of their work as "garden" or "landscape" that the two of them formulated in 1994 for the magazine *Topos* was largely coquettish: "We alternate between designing large landscapes or small parcels according to the commissions that come into the office." However, the relationship between their working planes is by no means restricted to the chances of the work situation. Linking the landscape element, which was increasingly equated with structure and function in the course of time, and the tranquil, locally restricted garden admittedly has always had a tactical significance for Desvigne and Dalnoky, but it also means something in terms of content and system. "To be recognized, our creative ability has to be expressed in the gardens, these highly regarded prototypes of landscape." And for their development as landscape architects this implies: designing gardens as a marketing offensive as well as a five-finger exercise in preparation for designing landscapes. And what about the development of

130

Competition entry for the Viaduc du Millau, France: interventions made while a motorway bridge was being built are organized in time-and-space-patterns along the existing landscape structures. Sets of scaffolding are placed as belvederes. When the construction work was finished the landscape seemed to have been *tidied up, rejuvenated, while the spatial structure remained the same.*

131 | 132

Jardin Caille, Lyon, France: this urban square in a residential area is organized in parallel bands made up of paths, planted areas, play strips, benches and lighting elements.

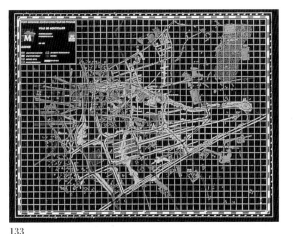

133

134

the garden? "We believe that the garden has no real spirit of its own until a piece of landscape crystallized within it, in all austerity." Tall birches as a green feature in the courtyard, for example. Planted like a little wood, they have straight-edged paths running between them with an avenue effect given by low lamps. Since then this birch motif has been repeated by many colleagues in many contexts.

"Now and again we come up with designs that fit in with our dream of a garden, because the image of an open landscape is expressed in them." This almost apologetic explanation is based on a paradox that they have perceived themselves: Desvigne and Dalnoky, who are so sceptical about gardens, discovered their specific interest in landscape in a garden. Both partners made drawings in the mysterious Renaissance garden of Bomarzo in Italy during their training in landscape architecture. They later returned to it as Villa Medici scholarship-holders, before founding their joint office in Paris in 1988. "It was while drawing in this garden that we decided to become landscape architects, in an architectural place in the midst of the Italian scenery. It was there we realized that gardens can be an artistic discipline of its own."

But gardens can be deceptive as well. For this reason Desvigne and Dalnoky have declared that the garden theme is taboo in current landscape architecture so long as gardens are merely equated with sweetness, charm, leisure and other atmospheric window-dressing. The garden stands for a deceitful aestheticization of the surroundings, a decorative snare, and a delusion. "Naïveté and an insufficiently critical approach are common in numerous publications about gardens – far more critical attitudes are taken to any other subject. But this banal discussion brings the modest and

133
Landscape design concept for Montpellier, France: starting with a design competition for the eastern access area to the town, the landscape architects were able to persuade the authorities to develop uniform design principles for the town as a whole.

134
Parc du Lez in Montpellier. The general guidelines continue into the town centre. The "key tree", the pine, is also used in a municipal park.

135

136   137

135 | 136 | 137
"A landscape that lasts two minutes."
Montpellier's eastern access area has a
striking backdrop of pine trees. The
change of perspective gives a sense of
travelling through the landscape.

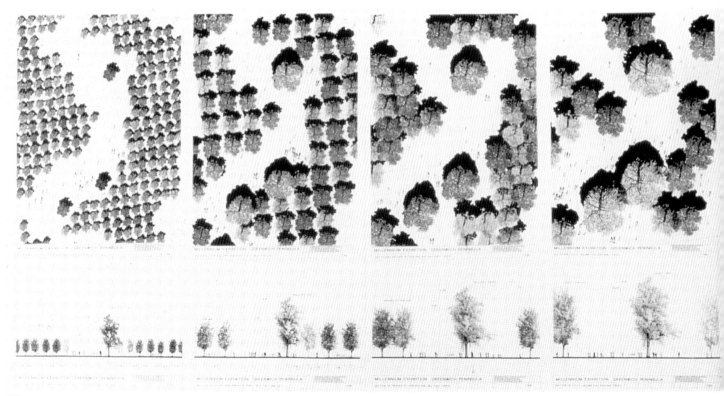

138

139

140

138 | 139
Greenwich Peninsula, London, Great Britain. The design concept for the site of the "Millennium Dome" and the "Millennium Exhibition" is based on planting large areas with trees.

The design radicalizes the idea of "tabula rasa". The interaction of sequence, cultivation and intervention from construction is generating a new landscape.

140
The peninsula was contaminated waste land until recently, and the topsoil had to be removed and cleaned. There was no possibility of relying on existing structures or historical strata.

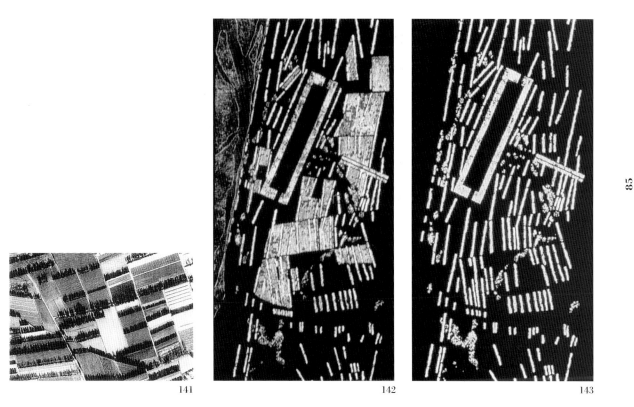

141   142   143

serious efforts that we make as landscape architects into disrepute. Once landscape architects had regained respect through their commitment in the field of landscape planning, it now seems as though the newly acquired knowledge and experiences of the past few decades have been swept away in a trice by the reactionary tendency to shift the garden as a prettified object back into the centre of interest. This is certainly comparable with the architects' cult of creating buildings that look like brooches, or the designers' cult of designing bodywork for cars in the form of aerodynamic equipment. None of this should be trusted."

Here distrust of the garden leads to enthusiasm for the landscaping experiment. This approach is based on a second paradox: "The European landscape has changed more in the past thirty years than in all the preceding period." Nothing new in this, as Michel Desvigne stresses. But he is disturbed by the part that landscape architects are playing in view of these increasingly fundamental changes. "Of course it is legitimate for European landscape architects faced with the scale of change in the landscape to dream of being involved in these processes. It is equally justifiable to claim an important social role for landscape architecture on the basis of these changes. But paradoxically this is not the case, this role does not exist." Desvigne and Dalnoky have put the marginal

141
TGV Méditerrannée, France: project to tie three stations on the high-speed TGV railway line into the landscape. Detail of the landscape prior to the project.

142 | 143
Structures like wind-protection plantations, fruit groves and avenues are used as the "original" that is quoted in the landscape design along the TGV line.

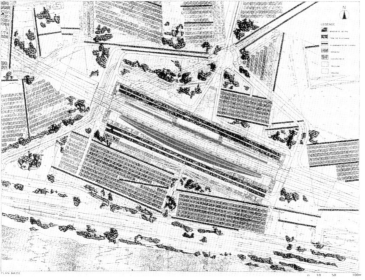

144

role of landscape architecture into figures: every French landscape architect works on an area per year corresponding to an eightieth of the land changed by forest fires, or a thousandth of the area that becomes urbanized. Working on these figures, it would take 2700 years merely to redesign the landscape of all the agricultural land that has currently been set aside. This significant game with numbers has a fundamental effect on conceptual attitudes. "In no case do our interventions have global significance or even a healing role. We neither define nor control the future of the landscape." It is essential to take note of this lack of meaning in order to find a productive approach to landscape architecture. "In some ways we are like a house-painter who has only one bucket of paint to cover a ten storey building. Under such circumstances it would be hopeless and wrong to try to paint the whole building. So the single bucket of paint has to be used for something else."

Desvigne and Dalnoky think that they have found a better use for the bucket of paint. Marginal interventions in particular should seem like works of art. People learn to look at their landscapes and the way in which they have developed in a new way. If you can't change the appearance of the landscape in a major way, you can at least influence the way in which people look at it. A marginal approach in terms of landscape and pleasure – this is the way the two of them define their work. "Changing a landscape is an enormous pleasure for a landscape architect." For this reason, things can definitely not be solved by falling back into a defensive position after identifying marginal significance. And yet this happens quite frequently. This reaction to changing the landscape is a "protective" reflex; action of any kind seems suspect to some landscape architects, and preservation becomes the central point of their argument.

144
Design for the Avignon TGV station.

145

146

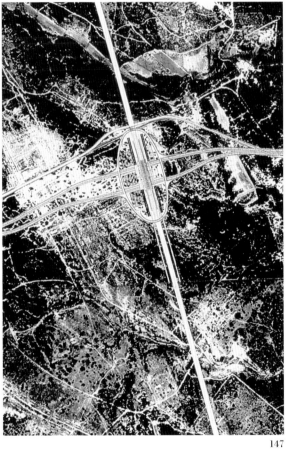

147

145
Model of the Avignon TGV station.

146
Plateau d'Arbois TGV station, Marseille: planned route for the track.

147
Fitting the TGV station into the landscape.

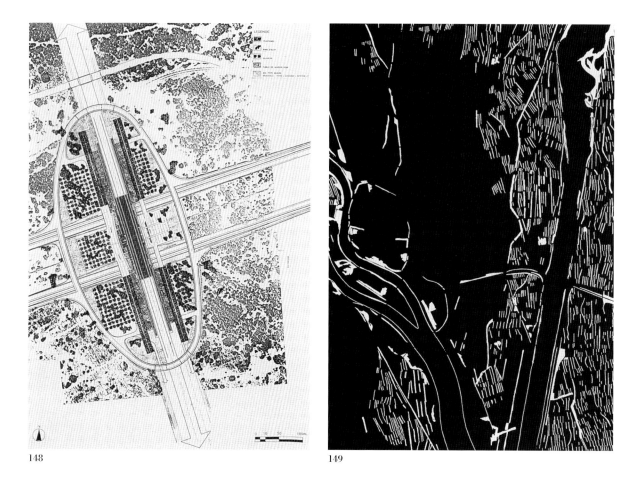

148

149

Desvigne and Dalnoky approach things differently: "We play with our landscapes and thus make forms that have to be created specially, and that are usually not taken seriously, meaningful and beautiful." They take the cue for their landscape-changing games from the present, the "century of communication". As knowledge about the nature that surrounds us is becoming more complex and at the same time more accessible, they feel that there is an incredible discrepancy between this contemporary knowledge and the survival of stereotypical images of gardens and landscape. It is both necessary and possible to detach ourselves from the traditional image, from the self-referential archetypes of landscape that have existed since the nineteenth century, in which the land is always hilly, water is always falling, nature is always intertwined. The vacuum between these old-fashioned images of landscape and strict formalism is what drives Desvigne and Dalnoky to produce new work.

148
Fitting the TGV station into the patterns of the surrounding vegetation.

149
Patterns of the surroundings.

"We do not want to imitate nature." The fascination of landscape does not lie in imitating forms, but in having insight into their development. The beauty of landscape is mathematical by nature, linked with thermodynamic processes and scientific laws. Thus merely reproducing forms is a backwards step in the face of insight, creating a dead piece of landscape, deprived of development.

Instead of this, Desvigne and Dalnoky influence developments by trying to avoid the trap of the complete landscape image. They achieve great effects with supposedly small interventions, appropriate to the landscape architecture of the future.

CHRISTINE DALNOKY and MICHEL DESVIGNE founded the DESVIGNE & DALNOKY practice in Paris in 1988.

Christine Dalnoky studied architecture at the Ecole nationale supérieure des Beaux-Arts in Paris and landscape architecture at the Ecole nationale du Paysage in Versailles. Michel Desvigne first studied botany and geology at the Faculté des Sciences in Lyon, before studying for a landscape architecture diploma in Versailles. This was followed by a phase of working with Michel Corajoud and Alexandre Chemetoff. A prize from the Académie de France in Rome took Dalnoky and Desvigne to the Villa Medici as scholarship-winners in 1986–87. After founding their joint practice, projects were realized in Belgium, France, Germany, Great Britain, Ireland, Italy, Japan, Spain, South Korea, Switzerland and the USA. Their best-known projects are the Millennium Park in Greenwich in co-operation with Richard Rogers, landscape design for three stations for TGV Méditerranée and open spaces for the Middelheim Sculpture Museum in Anvers, Belgium. Desvigne and Dalnoky work regularly with the architects Richard Rogers and Norman Foster.

Michel Desvigne has been a visiting professor in Lausanne, Geneva and most recently at Harvard. In 2000 he was invited as a visiting professor at the Architectural Association in London. Christine Dalnoky was visiting professor in Geneva in 1994–95 and since 1999. Both were invited as visiting professors at the Academia de Architectura in Mendrisio, Switzerland.

Desvigne and Dalnoky received the "2000 Award" of the French Academy of Architecture.

Contemporary European landscape architecture. What approach is it taking in the new century? If you look closely, you will find a number of trendsetting recent examples. The directions taken are very different. You will see landscape architecture as a way of helping towns and regions to define themselves, as a source of social and ecological renewal, working in partnership with architecture, which conversely is starting to devote itself to integrating buildings with the landscape, and above all landscape architecture as an artistically mediated reference to nature. This culture of landscape is an expression of advanced social awareness. Landscape architecture is being allotted the role of go-between for a new process of secularization. It conveys the idea of nature as defined by society – and we are insisting that this should be creative and not restorative: something new is to be created, it is not enough to restore the conditions of the past. In our current post-mechanistic and pluralist information and knowledge societies, landscape architecture has lost its function of copying generally accepted ideas about nature.

And yet: landscape gives a sense of direction, by definition. Traditionally, landmarks as elements of a scenery made it possible to gain a sense of where you were, and this is still the case today – sometimes with elaborate techni-

cal support. But landscape is more than a constructed image of topography: it is an aid to reading and describing a complex world. "Often artistic interventions reinforce the sign quality of landmarks; they emphasize their association with individuals and events and transform natural topography into a text that shows the way to those who can see, and at the same time enables them to see knowledge that has been handed down to us."[1] Landscapes and gardens function as a puzzle picture, somewhere between nature and art, supporting and mediating concrete conditions and abstract visions. It is precisely because nature and art are starting to dissolve into each other that landscape remains – as a code of complexity.

Landscape as a context mediates reality. Landscape architecture pursues the goal of reinforcing our experience by laying open the context. In the best case, landscape architecture creates impressions, signals ideas and sharpens the viewer's attention. In the very best, and very rare, case, a piece of landscape architecture manages to do everything at once – and all this in combination with the changing worlds of experience.

European landscape architecture has accepted the challenge of expressing how cultivated a society is – sometimes by partly questioning

1   KRAMER 1998

HANGLAGE MIT SEEBLICK. IN: KURSBUCH 131, NEUE
LANDSCHAFTEN, MARCH 1998, P. 11

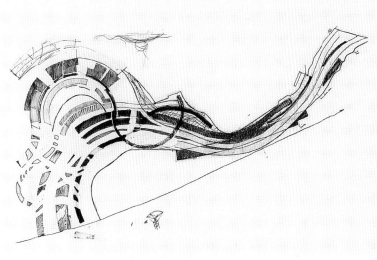

CODES OF COMPLEXITY

150
*Batlle i Roig: Parc Nus de
la Trinitat, Barcelona, Spain.
Design sketch 1990.*

these cultivated qualities. In this respect, landscapes and gardens represent a tension that triggers new experiences. They represent a society's development and future. At the same time landscape architecture is looking for its own ways into the future. Its past is ambiguous, its present diverse or at odds with itself – according to your point of view. But a glance at some outstanding examples of European architecture makes it possible to identify some principles that show historical continuity – despite all the changes.

Landscape as an Interpretation of Complexity

The modern concept "landscape" has come to mean much more than the pictorial quality of a Romantically coloured idea of landscape. Today "landscape" stands for the interplay within processes of self-organization, and thus, to put it more simply, for complex connections. For example, attempts are made to find laws for the growth of fractal urban landscapes by applying geometrical principles. Conversely, there are approaches both in the natural sciences and in philosophy to understanding apparently purposeful structures as the result of self-organized development processes that always remain formless in themselves, in other words processes which follow neither a cultural nor a biological programme as a defined final

form. Describing these process raises aesthetics as the science of sensory perception to a new level of significance, but one that is still based on aesthetic judgement and thus also on the history of the way in which landscape is perceived. Even in everyday language the idea of landscape is being applied increasingly descriptively – from the "political landscape" via "retail landscapes" to the "current economic landscape".

"Landscape" is now developing, if we leave aside the political and spatial and ultimately administrative source of the concept, via its aesthetic meaning, the image, into a cipher for a system, a code describing structures, abstract and removed from spatial categories. "Landscape" is becoming the expression of a way of looking at things that combines cause and effect, which links the seen image with the process by which it has come into being. The seeds of this can be found in hermeneutics as a discipline for critical description and also in synergetics, the consideration of principles of construction and structure, of the "living principles of form",[2] from the aspect of a complex system theory.

A change like this in the meaning of the concept of landscape – from consideration to description and then to explanation – is bound to

2 CRAMER 1994
     DAS SCHÖNE, DAS SCHRECKLICHE UND DAS
     ERHABENE. EINE CHAOTISCHE BETRACHTUNG DES
     LEBENDIGEN FORMPRINZIPS. IN: BIEN, GIL, WILKE
     (ED.) 1994: "NATUR" IM UMBRUCH, STUTTGART-
     BAD CANNSTATT

151

151
Lützow 7: Platz der Republik, Berlin, Germany. Competition entry 1997.

3 SIMMEL 1913

PHILOSOPHIE DER LANDSCHAFT. IN: DIE

GÜLDENKAMMER, NO. III, P. 635–644

affect landscape architecture. Certainly landscape architects are still working within the repertoire of the last two hundred years: Romanticism, scientific rationality and social identity determine the way in which they understand themselves and their work. But conceptual work is becoming more frequent. Landscape as an image-supported cipher and code becomes an interpretation in its own right instead of interpreting the representation of social attitudes.

The role of landscape architecture as applied art is still to process the aesthetic image of the landscape on a scale of 1:1, preceded by planning and design. In his 1913 essay *Philosophie der Landschaft* (The Philosophy of Landscape), Georg Simmel writes: "As complete human beings we stand before the landscape, both when it is natural and turned into art, and the act that creates it for us is immediately one of looking and feeling, broken down into these separate modes only in retrospect."[3] Here we can begin to see that landscape as mediated theory and as mediating practice no longer symbolizes only the unity of a whole, for example of a creation or of "nature", but is at the same time open to differentiated, thus to differentiating considerations. The idea of landscape, conveyed aesthetically, and at the same time explained scientifically and appropriated socially the world over, is in the throes of a change of meaning.

Of course the experience of landscape is not losing its significance, either in concrete or abstract terms. It is precisely its objective quality that induced and still induces us to continue developing the art and craft of handling landscape, its design, into a science of objectifiable connections. This is the consequence of a self-imposed compulsion to make insights scientifically concrete, and also a consequence of the possibilities offered by the scientific insights themselves. Geography, biology, chemistry and neurology are able to offer ever more credible hypotheses to explain the history of the earth and of nature, and of human consciousness, and they can simulate connections that cast their net ever wider. Landscape architecture cannot ignore this knowledge. In fact it is perfectly able in its own right to explain chains of cause and effect in the development of landscape, in other words the development of that concept of landscape that brings cause and effect together. Handling landscape is also a science to the extent that hypotheses can be formed, connections questioned and circumstances explained. The fact that counter-tendencies involving thinking back to landscape architecture as art are being formulated, propagated, discussed and implemented does not contradict this tendency to make things more scientific.

The idea of landscape as visible nature is supported by two fundamental sets of ideas that have developed in different directions: in the

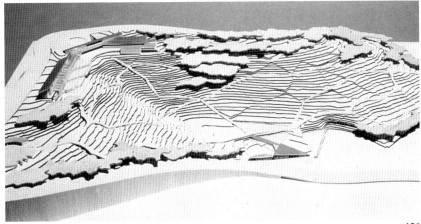

152

152
Bet Figueras: Nou Jardí Botànic,
Barcelona, Spain. Competition
model.

18th century landscape was seen as proof of the rational postulate of harmony – people felt that landscape that had been put to use was an expression of society's ability to regulate (itself), in contrast with the previously supposed destructive wildness of nature. "The rational unity of the cosmos found its aesthetic correlative in the visible unity of nature as landscape, i.e. as the apparent harmony of external nature."[4] In the late 18th and 19th centuries this rational perception of landscape became a Romantic one: Seen as natural beauty conveyed aesthetically, landscape represented the relationship between beautifully cultivated and sublimely wild nature. It became a Romantic compensation for the fact that society had lost nature, of the loss of the possibility of all-embracing, metaphysical patterns of meaning. These were also replaced by the modern empirical sciences.

Both the rational and the Romantic interpretations of the concept of landscape are still structurally effective. Feelings about landscape did not lose their significance under industrial Modernism in the 20th century. Landscape remains the province of landscape architecture, though now above all it quotes various ideas of landscape. The argument for the respective meanings involves social, political or ideological, aesthetic or scientific aspects, according to the particular interests. This is because the aesthetic, the social and the ecological identity of landscape architecture are all

consequences of the Enlightenment and of Modernism. These identities resurface in the ideas of the landscape garden, the people's park or the biotope.

These identities are so close together, indeed they sometimes overlap, and so it is scarcely possible to distinguish between them in many pieces of landscape architecture: landscape architecture's social line, often reduced to a functionally justified need for providing open spaces, to the ideology of light, air and sun for man as a working being, has similar sources to the ecological line, which goes back to the promise of salvation that came from the notion of a comprehensive science that would bring everything into harmony. These two turn-of-the-century approaches overlapped for a short time in the nineteen-seventies and early nineteen-eighties, when ecological questions were seen as more important in the heyday of the welfare state. Their existential and fundamental turn managed to put the force of law increasingly behind landscape architecture's approaches as part of the political ecology movement. Environmental awareness was expressed above all in local law, and for a time landscape architecture was absorbed into the canon of the administrative tasks of nature conservation and environmental protection.

Some of the recognition and significance accorded to landscape architecture today comes from this phase. But a fundamental ele-

4   SIEFERLE 1986

ENTSTEHUNG UND ZERSTÖRUNG DER LANDSCHAFT.

IN: SMUDA (ED.) 1986: LANDSCHAFT, FRANKFURT

AM MAIN

ment of Modernism, the aestheticization of the world we live in, the aesthetic debate, seems to have been lost to the socio-ecological plane of discourse. Landscape architecture has reacted to this; taking pleasure in designing seems to have taken over from ecological planning again. But seeing this as one trend taking over from another is deceptive, and not just because the presumed opposites come from the same source, or because of the more subtle nuances of reality. The principal reason is that the sociological question cannot be absorbed into the ecological one, and the two of them cannot be absorbed into the aesthetic question – and vice versa. If you look carefully at the development of landscape architecture, you will certainly be talking on the basis of inherently defined modes, but you will also be talking about changing challenges and tasks.

Thus it is neither necessary nor sensible to hope for a common identity for landscape architecture. On the contrary: landscape ar-

chitecture's potential does not lie in a unified profession, but in polarization. We should encourage controversy among landscape architects, rather than continuing to look for the one city, the only park, the overall ecological concept or the ultimate spatial image. But admitting contrasts, rather than harmonizing them, means that we have to recognize and show that it is possible to have opposing views against the search for harmony in landscape architecture.

Natures of Cultures

Generally speaking, landscape architecture is keen to emphasize the symbolic quality of landscape, to support it and in part to re-create it. Thus a design is always an explanatory, interpretative simplification of nature. "As the concept of Nature still has strong moral connotations and becomes the basis of actual planning, thus having concrete effects on the way we live, a critical reflexion on both our individual and the generally accepted attitude to nature is indispensable."[5]

5   WEILACHER 1996
BETWEEN LANDSCAPE ARCHITECTURE AND LAND
ART, BASEL, BERLIN, BOSTON

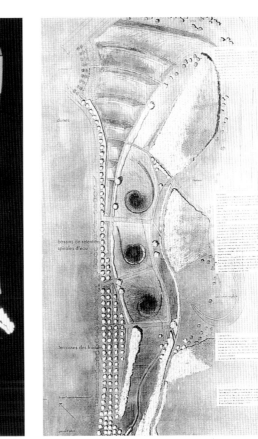

153

154

153
Desvigne & Dalnoky: tree species for the Greenwich Peninsula, Great Britain, 1997.

154
Latz + Partner: Europapark Luxembourg. Design 1994.

But this concept of nature is a very broad one: "Nature is not a category that can be unambiguously defined or even derived logically, but it is an object for consideration and an idea at the same time. (…) The meaning of the concept of nature is socially present in a range of associations, some of which run counter to each other. The idea about this object varies. First of all the idea creates the object; and yet it cannot be perceived independently from its object. This is because social reference to 'nature' moves between the ideal quality of nature and its material quality. And it is precisely in this field of tension that the idea of nature, the concept of nature, once more increasingly determines large areas of current discourse about the future of society."[6]

Keywords like "sustainability" guide our handling of landscape today. But here the same holds true: sustainability is always linked with exploitation. The dialectic of man and nature cannot be taken away, it can be seen as clearly in the most artful horticultural quotation as it can in a meadow full of wild flowers. "The scenery gains its perfection only in relation to man. However mightily nature and its primeval forms affect our spirit, and however much this quality may be preserved in the landscape for us, traces of human existence will always offer an agreeable addition to the sensations and thoughts that may be thus excited."[7]

As cultural assets, gardens and landscapes represent the greatest possible "simplification" of nature. The environment as cultivated by man is not just planted, tended, neglected, in short laid out and used more or less according to a plan. The environment, whether it is essentially urban or rural, Mediterranean or Alpine, wooded or bare, is cultivated because it is mediated by culture. Garden, park and landscape as we see them today are an expression of achieved levels of cultivation, of the culture of European society or societies.

6 SCHRÖDER 1997
NATUR ALS IDEE, FRANKFURT AM MAIN

7 LENNÉ AS CO-AUTHOR OF BETHE
ÜBER TRIFT- UND FELDPFLANZUNGEN, PRESENTED AS A LECTURE ON 8.5.1825, PUBLISHED IN 1826 IN THE VERHANDLUNGEN ZUR BEFÖRDERUNG DES GARTENBAUS IN DEN KÖNIGLICH PREUSSISCHEN STAATEN, P. 337

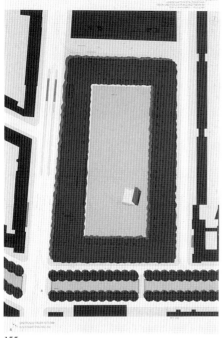

155

155
*Guido Hager: Platz der Einheit,
Potsdam, Germany. Competition
entry 1997.*

"Simplification" does not imply a reduced level of complexity here, although it is true that in a sense reduced complexity is an apposite description: the lawn as the highest level at which potentially natural vegetation can be repressed is indeed less complex than the latter. But the lawn as a horticultural task is an extremely complex structure: regular care has to be organized, nutrient supplies have to be controlled, and watering a lawn in summer is just as important for many lawns as keeping them warm in winter. A complex task, with the degree of complexity dependent on the extent to which the user of the lawn is bothered about it. And the relationship of social culture, i.e. sport, prestige, games, camping, mowing and raking by hand or mechanically, or simply being lazy, to the lawn as an object to be used is complex as well – but this is cultural complexity, related to a simplified natural condition. And our lawn is also the result of a decision to promote the growth of lawn grass and to keep other kinds out to as large an extent as possible. The lawn as expression of a decision entails an intellectual design. A lawn is a programme, and horticultural action is directed at carrying out this programme.

And so does landscape have a programme inherent in it? Landscape itself doesn't. Landscape architects derive their commission to design from this: from the need to give landscape a programme. A design does not traditionally function in any other way, in landscape architecture or in urban design, in politics or in philosophy: analysis, imagination, based on experiences, idea and decision. Then come scale, composition, material qualities.

Designers of landscapes, gardens, parks are looking for an idea (and sometimes also for a way of justifying it), in order to put a programme that is considered appropriate into practice. Appropriate in terms of the surroundings, the ideology, in terms of being entirely natural as far as planning is concerned, and ultimately in terms of taste. Design expresses an individual search for a principle that makes it possible to establish connections – once more a matter of mastering complexity by decision-making. The cultural achievement lies in simplifying nature, in influencing, i.e. interrupting natural processes on their way to something that in ecology is called a state of climax. Like everyone who influences nature, landscape

156

156
Agence Ter: Fondation Louis Jeantet,
Geneva, Switzerland. Competition
entry 1992.

architects are there to stave off climaxes. They justify this by creating cultural highlights – or so they claim. But the work of landscape architects, like any other cultural achievement, is not a substitute for nature, not a surrogate. And this precisely because what we call nature is nothing other than a social idea of nature, and thus itself a cultural product.

Landscape architecture has made a major contribution to developing our ideas of nature by planning the use of land and by designing parks and gardens. The idea of nature is not dependent on the effects of landscape architecture – the converse is more likely to be the case. But there is nothing that can be said about the present and future of landscape architecture without talking about the relationship between nature and culture. About a European relationship, an element of the Enlightenment that leads to the concept of "landscape" just as much as to concrete landscapes.

The Beautiful Picture
Until now, landscape architecture has only been able to capture part of the potential of landscape and express this in its work.

Landscape is beautiful, and thus an object of necessary pleasure – this has been the cultural consensus since the Enlightenment. Its formerly religious functions, for example as a "realm of evil" or – in contrast – "of the beautiful" –, as a threat or a promise, were replaced by the autonomy of art and along with this the autonomy of landscape art, in the spirit of the humane ideal. As the other side of reason, art mastered and masters myth, even by quoting myth. This principle defines the epoch of the Enlightenment, which is still happening now, and is thus at the same time a fundamental motivation for landscape design. Landscape architecture, as it perceives itself today, only became possible on the basis of the enlightened consensus on perception within the framework of aesthetics. The current spectrum of interpretations for the concept of landscape cannot be separated from the Enlightenment.

But at the same time, understanding landscape as a beautiful picture considerably restricts the potential of landscape architecture. The general pleasure taken in landscape, in the picture, leads here to ostensible harmony among those concerned with landscape architecture. People believe in their hunches about the meaning of landscape, and try to make them rather more scientific, while at the same time trying to make them impenetrable to any logic. There is scarcely any dissent in the profession about the meaning of landscape, or of its material qualities, or the idea behind it – and this is a disadvantage. When there are discussions about "landscape", they do not address its meaning, but the way in which it should be approached: is landscape a system, or at least part of a system, that can be controlled by definition, i.e. one that can be described with scientific precision? Or is landscape an expression of artistic or natural freedom?

The fundamentals are: as an "applied art", landscape architecture that is committed to an image, or picture, is particularly prone, like architecture itself, to being questioned about its social function. But landscape architecture, much more than fine art, has a specific dual function: landscape, in terms of both perception and design is both a cipher of liberation from a previously perceived natural condition and also a memory of this, of the idea of nature. Adorno's "uncertainty of the aesthetic wherefore" applies to landscape architecture not just as a (self)-questioning of its role, but above all as a challenge and a commitment to represent or transform social ideals. A municipal park expresses this challenge just as much as a Baroque garden, a natural garden just as much as an English landscape garden. These and other styles have in common that they create images of society, of the relationship between man and nature. Landscape remains part of the expressive potential of enlightened societies.

But the idea of landscape reaches beyond the image of landscape. The future of landscape architecture will also be defined by the question of whether the changed idea of landscape can be successfully approached.

Where does Landscape come from?
Landscape identity is always regional identity as well. From Sicily to Schleswig-Holstein, from Brittany to Berlin and Brandenburg, from Copenhagen to Catalonia there are similar problems, payments are made in the same currency and people are working on a European identity. But the landscapes remain diverse, and so do the geological, geographical and climatic influences – polar, Mediterranean or Alpine, and in between large areas with continental or maritime climates: the diversity of European cultures and their traditions is maintained in change. Thus regional identity is always cultural identity, conveyed by landscape: "landscape" is the quintessential cultural, socio-political definition of an area, a region, a picture.

157

158

157
Langenbach / Ivancsics:
Breitscheidplatz Berlin. Competition
entry 2000.

158
Gabriele G. Kiefer: "Schattenkino"
(Shadow Cinema). Installation,
Vienna, Austria, 1995.

8 THE OLD HIGH GERMAN WORD ‚LANTSCAF' MEANT
   AN "EXTENSIVE SETTLED AREA WITH UNIFORM
   SOCIAL AND LEGAL STANDARDS", SIMILARLY TO THE
   LATIN ‚PROVINCIA' AND ‚REGIO'. THE MIDDLE HIGH
   GERMAN ‚LANTSCHAFT' MEANT THE "TOTALITY OF
   INHABITANTS OF A COUNTRY/TERRITORY ABLE TO
   ACT POLITICALLY". CF. PIEPMEIER 1980: DAS ENDE
   DER ÄSTHETISCHEN KATEGORIE "LANDSCHAFT". IN:
   WESTFÄLISCHE FORSCHUNGEN, VOL. 30

9 SIEFERLE 1998
   DIE TOTALE LANDSCHAFT. IN: KURSBUCH 131, P. 157

10 IBID., P. 156 F.

This applies to the history of the concept[8] as much as to art history (early landscape painting shows, still without perspective, the unity of castle and working people) and also to the history of landscape: "the real landscape that observers have to deal with has for a long time not been 'natural' in the sense that it existed independently of human intervention."[9]

Now, if landscape "as the manifest totality of spatially extended reality" is not there in its own right but has to "rely on a preset understanding based on historical conditions",[10] then these conditions are the very ones that have been mentioned: 1. Landscape has become cultural landscape not just because of the way in which it has been cultivated in the course of time, but is a cultural dimension as such; 2. in Europe at least it does not make sense to distinguish between natural and cultural landscapes; 3. despite a general perception to the contrary, our cultural and historical image of landscape is not derived from the contrast between natural and cultivated landscape, expressed in everyday language as the contrast between town and country, but is an image of agricultural landscape; 4. this image changes with the real perception of landscape.

It is the prevailing image of agriculture that has caused us to equate regional and landscape identity. It is true that, because it has been shaped by human intervention, landscape is no longer natural landscape. Even European landscape painting used to show mainly cultivated landscapes, until its Romantic period. And yet – man's shaping of agricultural landscape was to a very large extent regionally specific and regionally differentiated. Restricted mobility and limited energy availability, scarce, regionally specific raw material deposits and different demands on buildings, exploitation methods and products arising from equipment, furnishings and climate led to regionally differing images in the pre-industrial landscape, which still affects our perceptions of landscape to this day.

Since then, in the course of the 20th century, landscape architecture has (again) left its regional and national points of reference behind. In the 18th century to an extent, and largely in the 19th century as well, models and stimuli for design were sought and found internationally: while travelling, from personal impressions, in literature and by concrete imitation. This is a result of new technical means for passing on knowledge and new horizons, brought about by constantly improving mobility and the new openness of enlightened societies.

The dawn of the 20th century was accompanied by optimistic visions of the future of mankind,

159
West 8: Schouwburgplein, Rotterdam, The Netherlands. Design 1990.

160
Rotzler Krebs Partner: "Augenweide" (Feast/Pasture for the Eye). 1998 design for the Federal Horticultural Show Potsdam 2001, Germany.

of internationalism, socialism and humanism based on global industrialization. At the same time landscape, in the form of the park, became a godsend when facing the social problems caused by industrialization in ever-expanding cities. "Light, air and sun", as well as the "sanitary green of the cities" (Martin Wagner) defined urban development and Modernism's concept of landscape.

Many of these visions were disappointed in the century of two world wars, the world-wide struggle between two political systems and numerous regional, nationalistic and ethnic conflicts, and to some extent also (re)classified as Utopias. Landscape architecture ceased to be something that conveyed an ideal image and became something that provided pre- and after-care, which was called caring for the landscape – a change that was reinforced by perception of an ecological crisis. In the meantime industrialism itself, in the form in which we knew it, was facing a fundamental change, indeed its very existence was questioned.

A Simultaneous Non-simultaneity
The International Style became accepted in landscape architecture in the course of the 20th century. This International Style, which was explicitly coined and cosseted by Modernism, was different from anything in pre-Modern Europe as it was no longer funded by and thus not dependent on the taste and understanding of individual patriarchs and rulers.

This means that any change of paradigm is less conspicuous in a democracy than in an autocracy. At the same time, dialectical Modernism always contains the counter-tendency within it, at least in embryo. For this reason we note stylistic changes only as slow evolutions that are perceived as fashions and yet influence our view of the world.

The International Style established its tastes freely, basing them not just on intellect and knowledge, but also on communication, criticism, exchange, on free access to information and knowledge. The 20th century was not just the century of Modernism, of an international quality in art and indeed in the art of gardening, on the contrary: explicitly anti-Modern counter-movements, with National Socialism in first place as exaggerated cultural conservatism and pessimism vis-à-vis internationalistic Modernism, rejected international approaches in landscape architecture and in art in general. Instead, landscape was identified with home, with regional identity in a nationalistic context. And yet the promise of Modernism remains the promise of the 20th century.

Because of historical ties, the dialectic of Modernism and anti-Modernism is still an element that helps to shape German landscape architecture in particular, while other countries, particularly The Netherlands and Denmark, see the traditions of international Modernism and those of recent nation history

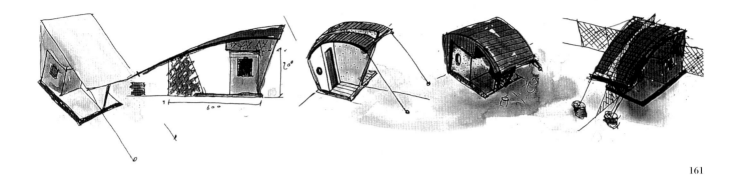

161

161
Agence Ilex: "Abris jardiniers"
(Equipment sheds for allotments),
France. Study 1993.

as congruent. For this reason, modern land-scape architecture in these two countries also shows the 20th century tradition, unbroken in its self-perception.

Despite these different developments in various European countries, modern landscape architecture in the International Style became a standard all over Europe. Crucial here were the nineteen-eighties and nineties, when the phase of discussion about the significance of public spaces (political and social discourse) moved into the phase in which work began on designing these spaces.

Equating modern landscape architecture with Modernism as a style will not provide adequate descriptions of all contemporary parks, gardens and landscape concepts. Design that is specific to a region, historical quotations and ideologies that are critical of Modernism all make themselves felt in modern landscape architecture, and so does the recently discovered aesthetic of waste or derelict land. But ultimately it was Modernism that established landscape architecture as a public rather than a merely private matter. Which meant that landscape architecture is now subject to public criticism.

Modernism is also rightly blamed for a temporary lack of meaning in landscape architecture. While abstraction began to take a hold in art, the garden (which was still concrete) start-

ed to fall behind. At the same time the theme of landscape as public space was subjected to administrative intentions. Landscape now added up to a series of functions that were and are to be emphasized in design. But in the meantime landscape architects had started trying to escape from the straitjacket of being functional: usually by making their work eclectically individual, but also increasingly by emphasizing the structural significance of landscape and the garden.

Landscape architecture is now an internationally inclined applied art again, and also an engineering science. In the last ten years in particular, the tendency for landscape architecture to be Europeanized at all levels from training via expert dialogue to publications has increasingly prevailed. Any major landscape architecture competition is now open to entries from all over Europe and has a jury with an international membership. It is striking that models chosen in an international context influence design in the individual European regions.

It is equally striking that landscape architecture is considerably enlarging its fields of activity as soon as a start has been made. An example: in Barcelona, a start was made in the nineteen-eighties on addressing the design of the city's public spaces (something that is now a model for many cities), and this triggered an interest in what landscape architects were

162

162
GROSS. MAX.: Regional Horti-
cultural Show Leverkusen,
Germany. Competition entry 2000.

doing elsewhere. For a few years Barcelona was a Mecca for landscape architects, and this launched a debate about designing public space in the landscape architects' home towns, and also discussions on training and the nature of the profession. It is not true only of Barcelona to say: "The concerns of landscape architecture extend far beyond urban design today. The problems of rural space and the urban periphery have been added on, and so have difficulties with infrastructure for cars and high-speed trains, and those of shopping malls and industrial estates, leisure landscapes and theme parks."[11] In other places people who were aware of all the problems faced by rural spaces had to rediscover the city as an area to be addressed by landscape architects. A simultaneous non-simultaneity.

This Europeanization has had a considerable effect on discussion about the issues involved in landscape architecture, and the course it should take. Ultimately its new significance is a consequence of the idea of Modernism: separating functions in urban development and architecture also drew attention to open space as a function, as a separate field of work intended to provide recreation and nature protection. Even though this development is starting to go into reverse today, with urban design,

architecture, landscape architecture, product and graphic design and art moving towards each other again in multi- or interdisciplinary working contexts,[12] the ideology of Modernism in particular, by separating functions, and therefore tasks, has helped to make landscape architecture more professional and to root it firmly in administration and law.

Signs for the Future

A European panorama: new urban design concepts seen through the eyes of landscape architecture (as urbanization is on the increase all over the world). Inner-city revitalization with new squares and parks. Discussion about new urban spaces – indoor and outdoor, Mall and Urban Entertainment Centre. Discussion about public, semi-public and private spaces, how to look after them, access to them. Addressing the subject of suburbs or housing estates, ways of working and living in the future. European cities and the New Urbanism. Converting former industrial and military areas. Derelict industrial land. Also re-naturalizing or re-cultivating large areas affected by mining. Or preserving gardens as historic monuments, in other words caring for and developing the heritage of one's own discipline. Commercial leisure areas (Center-Parks, golf courses etc.). But also urban ecology, sus-

11 VIDAL PLA
    IN TOPOS 27/1999, P. 42

12 IN ARCHITECTURE, FOR EXAMPLE, THERE IS AN
    INTENTION "TO TRANSLATE THE QUALITY OF A
    SPACE THAT IS CONTINUOUS AND AT THE SAME TIME
    HETEROGENEOUS INTO ARCHITECTURE (...) WHILE
    THE FLUENT SPACE OF CLASSICAL MODERNISM WAS
    CONCEIVED AS NEUTRAL AND HOMOGENEOUS,
    TODAY A HETEROGENEOUS CONTINUUM IS ESTAB-
    LISHED BY MEANS OF ARTIFICIAL TOPOGRAPHY."
    (OSWALT 1998: IMPLANTATIONEN. IN: ARCH+ 142,
    P. 76)

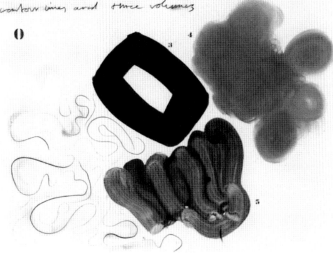

163

163
Stig L. Andersson: method sketch
"Contour lines and three volumes",
1998. Earth, lacquer, pastel and
graphite on cotton.

tainable development. Improving the image of towns by measures taken in their open spaces. Social green areas in cities, over and over again. Improving the residential areas' environments to the extent of creating new, high-quality and correspondingly profitable new sites and residential complexes. Designing meaningful surroundings for prestigious advertising purposes. And the job of preserving and developing non-urban cultivated areas with long traditions with changed uses of land and land management. All these are keywords in current debates that show the broad range of problems addressed by landscape architecture.

Ideas for solving these problems will lead to new landscapes, in the knowledge of new directions and possibilities. If the bipolar correspondence of nature and culture continues to break down, i.e. if the contrast is tending to disappear in the concrete cultivated landscape and also in the sciences and technologies that are increasingly linking natural and cultural processes, then "way(s) of looking at a world as a reciprocally heterogeneous concentrate of reality (will) be more in demand than ever".[13] What is "really" natural, what is "really" artificial? This question has always been contained in gardens and in the landscape as an object to be contemplated or to be designed. But certain-

ly they are both more valid as an associative description of this question than as an answer. Thus gardens and landscapes do not so much symbolize a crucial distinction as the indivisibility of the dual idea of nature as part and counterpart of man as a cultural being.

The parks and gardens that are being created today are pointing the way forward. Generally they are doing this in a way that is internationally intelligible and in the best cases they are advancing the cause of European landscape architecture. "The stimulating journey into the future began several decades ago, and the new contemporary garden is one of the places where the excitement of the experience is most evident."[14]

13 MELLITZER

QUOTED FROM ZENDRON 1999: GLOSSAR – ES IST

NATÜRLICH ALLES KÜNSTLICH. IN: KUNSTFORUM

145, P. 233

14 BORIANI 1996

LANDSCAPE DESIGN – LUXURY OR NECESSITY? IN:

THINK, INTERNET-FORUM BY EDITRICE ABITARE

SEGESTA SPA. (WWW.THINK.IT)

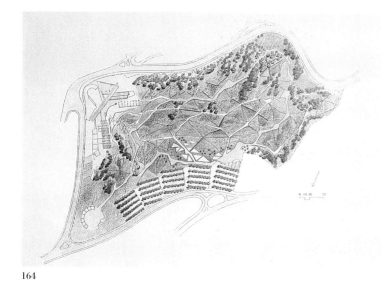

164

165

BET FIGUERAS

SENSUAL IMPRESSION

Bet Figueras designs sensitively and subtly. Plant, material and colour are brought together to make garden compositions that stimulate the senses. This landscape architect enters into an intimate relationship with the place that she is planning. Her aim is to use her craft to create a new relationship between place and material. This requires precise knowledge, and a feel for the spatial situation – right down to the last corner. This is why Bet Figueras particularly likes to design small, manageable sites: gardens occupying only a few square metres. A natural stone wall with a wild vine growing over it as a shared background for adjacent gardens. The organic shape of shrubs providing contrast in gardens with a rigid structure. Pines, hibiscus, wooden planks, geometrically laid floor coverings, pools – Bet Figueras sees the details of a garden as expressing its qualities. "Unlike large design commissions, the small ones are addressed or tackled as a whole. It is above all the materials that speak, the ones that are already there and the ones that are added."

But the new Botanical Garden in Barcelona proves that her attention to detail and sensitivity to a location can succeed on a larger scale as well. The city of Barcelona chose the site on the south-west slope of Montjuic, which is privileged in terms of its climate as well, so that Mediterranean plants

164
Nou Jardí Botànic, Barcelona, Spain: the 15 hectare New Botanical Garden is on the south-western slope on Montjuic, the hill in the southern part of the town.

165
The presentation of the plants is based on the seventy-two plant communities that occur naturally in the Mediterranean.

166

167

168

166
The structure of the garden is an abstraction of cultivated Mediterranean landscape. The landscape acquires a new, sculptural quality through the use of new materials.

167
The fractal landscape is continued in the architecture of the entrance buildings.

168
Walls of packed earth clad in Corten steel support the geometrical folds of the garden.

169

170

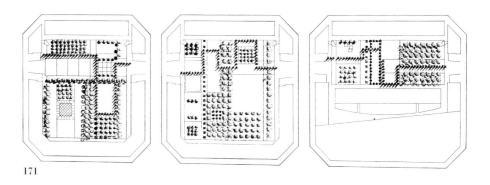

171

could make a particular impact as the essential theme of this park. Bet Figueras's design, which is particularly sensitive to theme and location, was elicited by an international competition. The Botanical Garden has now become a high point of contemporary European landscape architecture. And the fifteen hectare park is ideally suited to its predestined site on Barcelona's very own hill, which is increasingly dominated by modern architecture and landscape architecture, with a view over the city as a whole and the delta of the Llobregat river. And of course the task was in itself a temptation to a feast of design ideas. So what was produced is a piece of botanical education, a visual experience, a fascinating garden but above all a new kind of geometry for a sloping site.

The landscape architecture of the Botanical Garden is a story about the beauty of the Mediterranean landscape. Images of the Mediterranean scenery that are familiar because they are part of our collective memory are reinterpreted, above all the image of cultivated slopes with paths and tracks running through them. "As the spatial order was to take botanical requirements into due consideration, the articulation of the Gardens was to be largely determined by the distribution of plants, and given a basic geometric structure at the same time." (Figueras in *Topos* 29/1999) But

169 | 170
Sports formations are adopted for the areas inside the blocks in the Vila Olimpica, Barcelona. The materials and colours used for the floor coverings also take areas for sport as their theme.

171
The development of the Vila Olimpica is based on block grid of Cerdà's Eixample, which imposes shape on Barcelona. Geometry is interpreted playfully in the areas inside the blocks. A meandering band of poplars links the three blocks together.

172

173

172
*Jardí al Carrer Vidal i Quadras,
Barcelona: the contrast between grass
and natural stone as materials and a
sophisticated topography structures the
garden subtly.*

173
*Certain areas of the garden are made into
places in their own right, with the assis-
tance of the planting.*

174

175

the landscape architect is playing with the colours of the landscape as much as with geometry. The planting concept of this educational garden is new as well: Figueras does not present individual plants, but the Mediterranean's seventy-two plant communities, from aquatic plants via the macchia to mountain forests – a concept borrowed from the laws of ecology, illustrating interplay and connections.

So the landscape architecture tells a story of culture as well as nature in the Mediterranean. Figueras divided the whole site into unequal triangles – a fractal landscape as an abstraction of mature cultivated areas. The paths follow patterns laid down in the design. The site-mixed concrete covering for the paths picks up the basic triangular pattern. Broad joints make the irregular triangular shape of the concrete slabs stand out. On particularly steep slopes walls made up of soil that has been reinforced in layers and further protected with steel mats support the folds of the landscape. The walls are clad in Corten steel. They are reminiscent of the supporting walls in cultivated areas of the Mediterranean landscape. And the Corten steel blends in outstandingly well with the colour of the open soil. Yet the use of new materials does not make the landscape look theatrical and museum-like, but gives it a new sense of plasticity.

It is the combination of Mediterranean flora, geometrical shapes and the materials, which are particularly carefully chosen in terms of their colour, that makes Barcelona's new Botanical Garden into the epitome of Mediterranean landscape architecture, as a reminiscence of the cultivated landscape of the Mediterranean area. The architecture of the service buildings continues this staging of the landscape, which is based on fractal geometry.

174
Passeig de St. Fransesc, Barcelona (with Oscar Tusquets): lavishly planted clinker-brick access path.

175
A symmetrical pool of water, an olive tree and the huge pergola evoke associations with classical landscape painting.

176
The structure of the Carrer Abadessa d'Olzet garden in Barcelona is dominated by the central axis of the pool.

177
The surrounding parapet, supporting walls and the pool make the paths in the garden into a kind of labyrinth.

176

177

178

179

Playing with geometry is also the key to other gardens designed by Bet Figueras. One example is the Terrassa a Sarrià in Barcelona. You look out over the roofscape of Barcelona from the suburb of Sarrià – standing on top of a six-storey block of flats. The openness of the view and the intimacy of the space had to be combined in the roof terrace design. Bet Figueras put together wooden planks, strewn gravel with hibiscus and geraniums planted in terra-cotta pots, and wooden tubs for orange trees and date palms. The sequence of spaces corresponds with the architectural pattern of the building underneath. Figueras conveys the privilege of living above the city with a quotation from cultural history: a pool of water evokes memories of the coolness and tranquility of a Moorish garden. "The splashing of the water, the fragrance and colour of the plants, transport the residents into another world – far away from the imposing city. But contact with the city is not disturbing, on the contrary, it is made the more valuable by the extraordinary perspective." The roof becomes an urban oasis.

Water is even more important in the Jardí al Carrer Abadessa d'Olzet, another private garden in Barcelona. The garden façade of the new building is reflected by day or night in a long pool of water that relates to its symmetrical articulation, and the pool then dominates the symmetrical garden. It is this play with the architecture of the building in the related garden that makes Bet Figueras's design so distinctive.

But geometry is built into the Jardí al Carrer Vidal i Quadras much more reticently. This site on the periphery of Barcelona is much broader, and highlighted by glimpses of the surrounding area. Here it was enough to emphasize the slight slope on the site with a few terracing steps down towards the pool. The individual steps are framed and patterned quite severely in stone. Grass and a small number of trees allow the garden to flow with a pleasing generosity that suits the area.

178
The surface of the water as a mirror for
architecture, vegetation and the sky.

179
The architecture is reflected in the corresponding garden.

180

181

Figueras designed the courtyards – Jardí interiors – for the Barcelona Vila Olimpica differently again, but again with clearly geometrical handwriting. Here plant formations, above all the tree planting, support the asymmetrical geometry of the gardens. Once more water provides highlights for the architecture, to which all Bet Figueras's gardens relate closely, sometimes as a pool that can be used, sometimes as a visual effect, a reflection. And yet the garden is not a reduced image of the buildings around it, but a theme in its own right. In the case of the gardens in the Vila Olimpica, sports formations are translated into abstract gardens.

And so ultimately it is not just intimate knowledge of the places for which she is designing, not just her love of geometry and plants, that inspire Bet Figueras's gardens and parks, but a theme as well, a narrative. This is how landscape architecture is produced and woven with sensitivity and subtlety.

180
A roof terrace in the Sarrià district of Barcelona is both an urban place and a private privilege. The spatial sequence corresponds with the architectural pattern of the building underneath.

181
Awnings and date palms to provide shade, orange trees and hibiscus in tubs create a private world high above the city.

182

183

182
This garden by the sea thrives on its unique position. The contemplative atmosphere is enhanced by the interplay of existing vegetation and the architectural elements.

183
The clear separation between the individual areas of this block interior in Barcelona gives the design the quality of a piece of abstract graphic art.

184

185

BET FIGUERAS I PONSA born 1957 in Barcelona, studied landscape architecture at the University of California in Berkeley, at Georgetown University in Washington and at the University of Edinburgh. She founded the "Arquitectura des paisatge" office in Barcelona in 1983, and started teaching landscape architecture at the Escuela Técnica de Agricultura, Barcelona, in the same year.

Her most important projects, alongside some planting concepts and landscape development studies have been a large number of private and public gardens and parks. Bet Figueras has realized gardens, parks and squares in France and Japan, and above all in Spain. Outstanding among these are the Terrassa a Sarrià roof terrace, the Jardí al Carrer Abadessa D´Olzet (with Oscar Tusquets, Architect), the Jardí al Carrer Vidal i Quadras (with Tonet Sunyer, Architects), the Jardí interiors de Tres Illes a la Vila Olimpica (with Carlos Ferrater, Architect) and the Jardí de

L'Illa Diagonal, with architects Manuel de Sola Morales and José Rafael Moneo, all in Barcelona; the area around the Simon a Olot factory, Girona (with Lluis Clotet, Architect), the area around the Public Library in Seville (with Cruz & Ortiz, Architects) and the New Botanical Garden in Barcelona (with Carlos Ferrater and Josep Luis Canosa, Architects).

186

184
A sequence of dry areas and pools of water in the Can Misser garden, Spain (with Oscar Tusquets) plays with the typically Mediterranean motif of terracing.

185
The interplay of light and shade, of architectural elements and vegetation and of open and close spaces contribute to the charm of this garden.

186
The square elements of the Jardí de la Casa del Prior, Spain (with Maria Jover): the symmetrical ground plan of the garden relates to old monastery gardens. Yew hedges edge the garden area. The wisteria-covered pergola at the end offers a place for quiet contemplation.

CREATING BEAUTIFUL THINGS

Guido Hager trusts plants. Hager is a landscape architect who is still first and foremost a gardener and botanist. And he is a landscape architect who loves gardens. There is scarcely anyone else who develops work, and particularly work for public spaces, so clearly from a passion for gardening, by putting the beauty of the project in hand before anything else.

Many of Hager's designs have proved that gardens and plants can express their beauty in luxuriance, but do not have to. His extremely simple design for the Platz der Einheit in Potsdam places a columned hall of lime trees in three rows around a lawn. This centrally placed lawn, a step lower than the surrounding level of the town, is the simplest form of garden. The only highlight is a pane of blue glass. This glass sculpture is as high as a building, and accessible, and symbolizes the former Potsdam synagogue: an *aha* that catches the eye, and that could not sustain, and does not need, any distractions.

It is the strength of their supposedly gentle provocation that makes Hager's designs into something special. Provocation using the resources available to a gardener? Hager wants to create something beautiful, and at the same time shows a sense of history and respect for the location. This is not a contradiction for him, though it is for others. Clients, jury-members, professional colleagues, they all like a statement to be made: a square – paved, a garden – with flowers. People like to know what they are dealing with.

Guido Hager addresses precisely this either-or without taking sides. This landscape architect has provided his own answer to Adorno's question about whether it is possible to write a poem after Auschwitz. Gardens are in the tradition of the beautiful, and he cannot and will not deny this tradition. And so he intends to develop it further, and is perfectly capable of doing this. This alone is enough to make garden-lover Guido Hager into an *agent provocateur*. He quite simply loves gardens, but historical gardens in particular. For this reason above all garden monument conservationists react to his work with great scepticism. "Many of the garden conservation commissions that my office has won were supposed to be carried out on the basis of reconstruction – but always with various up-to-date technical additions. After detailed study of the gardens and the archives we have usually come down on the side of developing the design, as reconstruction on the basis of mea-

187

188

189

187
Country House in Grafenort, Switzer-
land: the original design for the Baroque
garden cannot be established, either from
the archives, or by excavation. Hence
Hager's design is a new interpretation.
Walls that were still in evidence were
refurbished and completed.

188
The building is used as a holiday home
for monks and as a conference centre.
Flowerbeds placed in front of the façade
take up the geometry of the house.

189
The garden becomes an element connect-
ing house and surrounding landscape.

191

192

193

GUIDO HAGER

190

The two garden levels were given gravelled areas and inscribed square lawns.

191

Swisscom Building, Binz, Zurich, Switzerland: the open spaces are on the site of a clay-pit that was used as a rubbish dump for a time. The slopes of the pit are now a nature conservation area. Surface water must not soak away, but has to be drained off on the surface.

192 | 193

The design is close to nature, with pools for retaining and evaporating water creating a number of biotopes. But an artificial language is used that is appropriate to the artificial nature of the place.

194

195

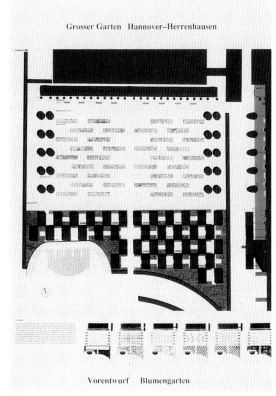

Grosser Garten Hannover–Herrenhausen

Vorentwurf Blumengarten

196

197

194 | 195
The flower garden at the Baroque palace of Herrenhausen in Hanover, Germany has been returned to its original function after being used for catering purposes for 30 years.

196
The spatial and horticultural structure is derived from naïve carpet patterns, which are both elementary and at the same time individual.

197
A contemporary interpretation of the "parterre à pièces coupées". This flower-bed is made up of thirty-six beds fringed with box hedges. A sea of flowers is planted twice a year.

gre sources and the desired technical adaptations did not seem to make sense in terms of garden monument conservation. We often lost jobs as a reaction to this. But some clients accepted our approach of fitting contemporary design into the historic garden. And now people actually ask us to make contemporary additions to historical gardens."

Gardens can have value as monuments. Hager is at pains to point this out. But he feels that treating a garden merely as a monument is to undervalue it. And this is exactly why Hager is a sensitive artist when it comes to handling historical sites, and an interpreter who enriches the history of horticulture, constantly adding new chapters. An artist? Hager resists this. He sees himself as a landscape architect, and he would also accept the term "garden artist". But artists, who increasingly turn to the garden as a subject, though often with dubious results, have a different role and different possibilities available to them. They have "the advantage of free access" over landscape architects. "But we landscape architects are restricted, restricted by the traditions of horticulture, by ecology, by the usefulness and sustainability of everything we design, construct and plant."

Guido Hager sees these commitments as a privilege rather than a burden. "Horticulture, garden art, is an applied art. As a gardener I have to be interested in how my work will grow over the decades. But as an artist, especially in Concept Art, Pop Art and Land Art, I am interested in how a garden is presented, in landscape as a work of art, as a presentation for the moment. This is why works by "artists as gardeners" – the subject of a special edition of the magazine *Kunstforum International*, vols. 145 and 146/1999 – often seem banal when they are considered as gardens. It is the privileged "risk of transience" that landscape artists are taking when working with living plants. For artists this risk exists only on the level of perception.

Hager plants, he constructs gardens, he designs using natural forms. His work always makes the impression of being artificial, self-conscious and produced with awareness of the traditions of horticulture. So he lays out his flowerbeds outside a large house in Grafenort in Switzerland on a grid pattern that reflects the geometry of the house. This new garden geometry interprets the earlier Baroque garden: abstract forms, composed from natural forms. "Plants are becoming increasingly important to me as building materials. I use other materials, artificial structures, less and less frequently." Hager is well aware of the risk that he is taking with plants as building material. "As I use plants as material, I have to intervene more frequently and more intensively. Plants have to grow, they have to be tended and pruned regularly." Cultivation techniques that other landscape architects no longer rate highly. Or it may be that colleagues are not as knowledgeable.

Hager can be provocative, but not for provocation's sake. He simply states the demands he makes on his own work as on landscape architecture in general. And it is for this reason in particular that this reticent innovator has got into the bad books of some garden monument conservationists. But there the landscape architect is only pointing particularly clearly to a special difficulty posed by garden monument conservation: if a garden goes into decline as interest in it decreases, then it should be allowed to go into decline. Without trace. But if interest remains, or if it revives decades or centuries later, reconstruction is attempted as much as possible. Often people dip into an epoch at random, without any knowledge of the time-scale on which way the garden has grown and then passed away, so that this can be shown to the world of here and now as the correct condition the garden should be in: timeless, without breaks between the old and the new, and so rather like a stage set. Hager sets his own approach against this, with his own, up-to-date contribution.

Hager's essay "Against Reconstruction" (cf. *Topos* 19) was published in 1997. He still sees this text as a key statement and expression of the way he sees himself: "A park can gain authenticity if something is added or constructed with the old. The antiquity of the garden monument will not depreciate in value. Instead, working on the historic grounds once again becomes a creative act. [...] Of course every addition creates a break between the old and the new. But our world is full of breaks and we must acknowledge them in historic parks as well – without losing sight of the park as a

198

198
The Rechberggarten in Zurich dates from the second half of the 18th century. It was once one of the most magnificent Baroque gardens in the city, and has been redesigned frequently since it was first laid out. It was most recently used by the university, and has been open to the public again since 1992. Bedding plants, spring 1995.

whole. The park should not turn into a series of ruptures but a new, if not heterogeneous, integrated whole." Hager fears that the reconstruction approach will bring horticulture to a standstill. The very man who so likes looking back into the history of garden art would like to see a more courageous approach to features of the present and the future.

On the whole, garden conservationists rejected and refused to tolerate this approach. But Hager has acquired a more distinctive image. And he knows that his attitude puts him on the side of the most important architects who deal with historic building stock. "Monument conservationists scorn the reconstruction of buildings. But the redevelopment of historical buildings is an everyday event. Think of Karljosef Schattner's buildings in the old town in Eichstätt. But reconstruction is customary in garden monument conservation. Have we no confidence in the future of landscape architecture? Or does constantly dealing with the work, the cultivation that is constantly needed to do this, entice us into always wanting to restore gardens to their original condition? But what actually is the original condition of an old garden?"

Guido Hager is well versed in garden conservation work. His office has produced a large number of reports and care manuals for historic gardens. The Rechberggarten is one of the city of Zurich's most magnificent Baroque gardens, and it has often been redesigned. Hager protected and refur-

199

200

201

199
The walls, banked lawns and trees are important for reasons of monument conservation. They have been retained and refurbished as original stock from various development phases.

200
The University of Zurich is involved in planting out and tending the bedding plant scheme, which is redisigned annually by Nicole Newmark.

201
Bedding plants, summer 1996.

bished the walls, banked lawns and trees that are so important by monument conservation standards to the various construction stages. But he went for the complementary principle: additional structures and planting "complement" the garden "on this historical model", but in contemporary language. "Horticulture between preserving and inventing something new" was praise from the *Neue Zürcher Zeitung*. This garden has acquired a very different purpose from the one it served in the second half of the 18th century. It is now open to the public, it is a beautiful ornamental garden, a place for relaxing in the city centre. "This garden tells us about old Zurich and changing garden fashions." Right down to the present day. And so the bedding plant scheme is redesigned annually to ideas by Nicole Newmark, a level of horticultural lavishness that is possible only because the University nurseries are to hand. And it is an effort that keeps the Rechberggarten alive.

The Rechberggarten is a tribute to beauty produced by lavish use of bedding plants. Diversity with the changing seasons. Horticulture wants to live as well. For horticulture brings us closer to nature. "We are looking for artefacts that can be transformed into idylls with the passage of time."

202

203

204

202 | 203
Additional structures and planting
complete the garden in contemporary
language, following the historical model.
Bedding plants, summer 1997.

204
Red and white patterned wooden tubs
with palms, agaves, lemon and laurel
trees, complemented by modern red
benches.

GUIDO HAGER, born 1958, trained as a landscape gardener and then as a botanist. He studied landscape architecture at the Hochschule Rapperswil from 1981 to 1984. He has worked as a self-employed landscape architect in Zurich since 1984.

Hager and his staff of eight produce expert reports on garden monument care, plan and design new additions to historic gardens, and also for contemporary ones. Hager submits his views on garden monument conservation to a number of professional and specialist associations, and to the Swiss Monument Conservation Commission. Hager regularly teaches and works as an assistant at the ETH Zürich. Success in international competitions and invitations to take part in conferences and sit on prize juries have carried his reputation far beyond Switzerland.

Hager's most important projects are the modern garden for the Swisscom Building, Zurich (1988–94), the play-park on the Schärrerwiese, Zurich (1989–91), second prize in the competition for Platz der Einheit, Potsdam 1997, landscaping for housing at Limmatwest, Zurich (1996–2001), the Hirschgraben garden, Zurich (1989–92), Wohnanlage Mc Nair, Berlin-Steglitz (1997–2002). The Hager office has devised park care and new designs for sites including the Rechberggarten, Zurich (from 1986), the Liguster school building, Zurich (1987–92), the Baroque garden at Grafenort (1994–95), the St. Katharinental monastery garden, Diessenhofen (1994–95), the Baroque garden of Kleiner Türligarten, Chur (1994–95) and the flower and fig gardens at Herrenhausen in Hanover (1996–99).

205

206

207

205
Bedding plants, summer 1998.

206
The juxtaposition of different historical strata makes the Rechberggarten into a place that tells a story of old Zurich and changing horticultural fashions.

207
Bedding plants, summer 1999.

208

HEIKE LANGENBACH / ROMAN IVANCSICS

RATIONALITY AND POETRY

Heike Langenbach and Roman Ivancsics give a new structure to public space by designing it in recognizable gradations of urban quality. They emphasize the independence of the squares and gardens that they design. Their aim is to create places that are all identifiable in their own right, rather than a monotonous sequence of buildings and spaces between them. Simple, and thus clearly recognizable, structures reinforce the identity of the places through their authenticity, which is based on design principles, rather than showiness. Langenbach and Ivancsics allow themselves to be guided by ideas of Modernism and by the precise qualities of craftsmanship.

209

210

211

208
Square in front of the Austria Tabak cultural centre, Vienna, Austria. The artificial urban landscape was created in cooperation with artist Leo Zogmayer.

209 | 210
Tectonics. Height differences measured in centimetres are enough for precisely placed topography.

211
The lettering "JETZT" (Now) looks as though is has been chiselled out of the slope.

212

213

214

212 | 213
Residential open space in the Marzahn prefab housing estate, Berlin, Germany. The estate's design language is not negated, but confidently taken up and continued in the external areas.

214
Barnimplatz, Marzahn. Walls, steps and benches, design elements in the neighbouring residential open space, are taken up in the public square.

The practice has realized key projects both in inner-city districts and also on large and small suburban housing estates. The basis of their design approach is that they avoid simulation. They will not have any truck with markedly historical or *Zeitgeist*-related design elements: they do not create areas of marshland in back yards or granite hills on playgrounds, and they do not use nineteenth century chandeliers for contemporary housing estates. When they create a square in a mass housing estate, they do not negate the architectural design language, but self-confidently take it up and carry it forward. In place where landscape and plants dominate in suburban surroundings, they assign a particular role to gardens. Thus every place is made special by design for its open spaces that is entirely appropriate to that place.

Langenbach and Ivancsics cultivate a simple and reduced design language in their choice of forms and materials, which leads to results that end up all the more powerful and elegant. "Our aim is elegance achieved by minimal and modest means. Landscape does not need massive gestures to give it quality. We want to show that civil and building engineering and solid craftsmanship are more to be trusted than fashionable developments in style. Care and simplicity in the use of resources and materials are among the best opportunities to create an approach to garden art that a large proportion of our society can identify with."

It is generally acknowledged that these landscape architects, based in Vienna and Berlin, have little if anything to do with the *zeitgeist* that dominates today's international landscape architecture scene. But while many practices insist that their work should constantly catch up and conform, Langenbach and Ivancsics have developed a design approach that is entirely their own. Their work is praised for the "clear logic of a calm and unspectacular design" (*Zolltexte* 21/1996). The special quality of their designs derives from "knowledge of the location and its general conditions". But what some people see as an "almost perfect example of diplomacy in landscape planning" (ibid.), as handling whatever situation is found diplomatically, is resisted by others.

Heike Langenbach met with resistance of this kind after realizing an appropriate and exquisitely designed square, Barnimplatz, for a large housing estate in Berlin, and was then ticked off by some people for an absence of *Gemütlichkeit* inherent in the *genius loci*. But the lucidity of the place is praised in expert circles, and Barnimplatz with its minimalist highlights seen as a "new concept that points the way forward" (cf. *Jahrbuch Architektur in Berlin* 1997, Biennale Barcelona 1999).

215

Langenbach and Ivancsics regulate the romanticizing effect of green backdrops by their interest in urban space, in the urban quality of squares and parks, which does not exclude respect for gardens as part of the city. "The poetic quality of our projects is not immediately apparent because it is captured in the logic of a calm, precise design." Elements that structure or accentuate space are important. Walls, steps, water, trimmed hedges and groups of trees: vegetation is also an architectural element, and is placed geometrically. And yet the geometry of their projects is not an end in itself, but secures a link with the location. Langenbach and Ivancsics are concerned to anchor the open space they design in the surrounding area. Thus in the Park am Leberberg, in Vienna, the geometry of the place was derived from old field and parcel structures, but also from the way in which the park related to the city around it. This means that the park is closely tied in with the city in terms of its function as well as its design. "The crucial factor is that we always work from the basic atmosphere of the place as we find it, which we interpret and develop further. This is not least a rational and analytical process. We keep anything good; we intensify anything usable; anything unusable we reformulate."

But at the same time the landscape architects stress the poetry of the garden: "For us gardens are spaces intended for contemplation, for bringing together, and at the same time for overcoming the dialectic of thinking and feeling. We feel that a slowly developing garden can be up-to-date without being modish. It is not least a poetic space. This poetry is achieved not by poetic objects, but by specifically rejecting them. A space becomes a poetic place as a result of consistent reduction, through simplicity and precision. To that extent we aim to combine complexity in terms of content with formal simplicity."

215 | 216
Sculpturally shaped walls function as steps or bridges. They mark caesuras in the space and form a basic framework for the actual theme, the gaps.

HEIKE LANGENBACH / ROMAN IVANCSICS

217

218

219

220

221

217
Felmayer Gärten, Vienna. The hedge planting is so arranged that it enhances the spatial depth of the space.

218
The suburban character of the place is taken up by emphasizing its scenic features. Simple structural elements, used with precision, define thresholds and passages.

219 | 220 | 221
Plants convey mood and atmosphere in the Felmayer gardens (in cooperation with Cordula Loidl-Reisch).

Thus there are levels in Langenbach and Ivancsics's projects that are not immediately intelligible. Plants usually play a crucial part. "We use plants in our projects to create moods and atmospheres. Almost all our gardens have romantic associations as well, which are always deliberately built into the plant spectrum. We even placed a sea of wild flowers and fruit trees between Berlin's rough mass housing estates."

A contradiction between a Romantic approach and Modernism? Langenbach and Ivancsics deny this, and identify a design principle that is common to both: "We have learned something from Luis Barragán: what is needed to create landscape that does not resist its architectural surroundings is above all a very marked sense of simplicity: abstract quality, straight lines and precise surfaces. We have learned from the history of garden art that a poetic garden space does not derive from specific stylistic and design characteristics, but results from placing lines, surfaces and bodies precisely." Hence plants are used in the form of trimmed hedges, rows of trees or space-creating cubes, when herbaceous borders are not called for. Concrete is also used as up-to-date technology, seen by the landscape architects as a conceptual and technological challenge. But Langenbach and Ivancsics know how to use concrete, confident of quality and themselves, as a 'high-grade material'.

In their projects Langenbach and Ivancsics urbanize the suburbs by offering new symbols that create identity. One example is the use of walls. "The wall as the oldest and perhaps most venerable element of garden architecture often has a crucial part to play in our squares, parks and gardens, sometimes simply for technical reasons, because we have to shore up a slope, for example. We try to make that into a theme as well. Used as steps, bridges, as a threshold or caesura or as a sculpture and landmark, walls are thus often building-bricks in our tectonic concept for the piece of land that we have found. Walls create special places and special intimacy. They form the basic framework for developing the spaces and gaps that are our actual theme. This is probably expressed most clearly in our squares."

Langenbach and Ivancsics see wall and space as just as much of a dialectical combination as rationality and poetry. For this reason they emphasize the transitions in spaces that have been addressed rationally and make a poetic effect. "Often very little is needed to formulate a transition in this way. We know from gestalt psychology and 20th century art that a form can be recognized from a few strokes. And so all we did in a garden with a fine stock of old trees was to place a few hedges in geometrical rows. There is a paving slab in the openings between the hedges. That is enough to tell walkers that that they are entering a different space."

222

222
Park am Leberberg, Vienna. The wall, the oldest and perhaps the most venerable element in landscape architecture, is used as both a structural-technical and an aesthetic element in many designs.

Subliminal differentiations of this kind can be seen in many of their projects. "On the whole there is too much use of materials in recent landscape architecture." Their use of concrete or natural stone testifies to the functional and aesthetic qualities of these materials, precisely in their contrast with the plants. It is this quality of contrast in particular that makes the necessary gradations of urban and artificial quality visible vis-à-vis a rural quality as something supposedly natural. But this contrast is not an end in itself. It is intended to introduce a sense of comprehensible order into the places. The key is that we are invited to find our way, to get our bearings as a result of the lucidity of the design and the way the space is shaped.

Heike Langenbach and Roman Ivancsics define landscape as space, as surroundings that in turn shape the surroundings and are shaped by them. Anyone who withdraws from this dialectical relationship replaces necessary distinctions with false images of unambiguity and thus negates landscape architecture's cultural role.

223

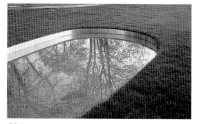

224

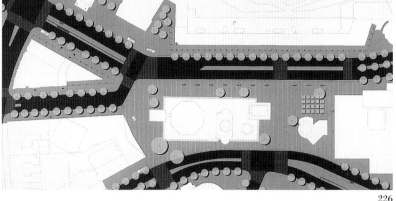

225

226

HEIKE LANGENBACH and ROMAN IVANCSICS work as landscape
architects in Vienna and Berlin. Heike Langenbach was
awarded her landscape planning diploma at the Technische
Universität in Berlin in 1983, and after this worked there
as a scientific assistant. Since 1997 she has taught at the
Technische Universität in Vienna. Langenbach opened her
Berlin office in 1983.

She has been working with Roman Ivancsics since 1990. He
was awarded his diploma at the Universität für Boden-
kultur in Vienna in 1981. Ivancsics taught there from 1982
to 1987, and at the Technische Universität in Vienna from
1994. Ivancsics opened his own office in Vienna in 1982.

Heike Langenbach and Roman Ivancsics's work comprises
both large-scale projects and smaller operations. They produced green-space concepts for large urban extension areas
in Berlin (e.g. Wasserstadt Oberhavel) and Vienna (e.g.

Donau-City, Aspern airfield area). They won competitions
for the municipal park Am Urbanhafen, Berlin in 1990, for
the Felmayer Gärten park, Vienna in 1990 (with Cordula
Loidl-Reisch), for the external facilities at Wittenberger
Straße and Barnimplatz, Berlin in 1993, for the Park am
Leberberg, Vienna in 1995, for the Vienna-Hirschstetten
green belt in 1996, for the square in front of Austria Tabak
Cultural Centre, Vienna in 1999 (with Leo Zogmayer) and
for Breitscheidplatz, Berlin in 2000, and most of these have
been realized. Langenbach and Ivancsics worked with
architects like Norman Foster, Christoph Langhof and
Hans Kollhoff & Helga Timmermann on the external facilities for the Artistensporthalle, Berlin, for the Leibniz-
kolonnaden, Berlin and for various residential developments in Berlin and Vienna.

223 | 224
STO AG park, Berlin. "The space is con-
densed to become a poetic place by consis-
tent reduction, simplicity and precision."

225 | 226
Breitscheidplatz, Berlin. Competition
entry, 2000. Bands of light are let into the
ground and re-interpret this urban loca-
tion.

227   228   229

CORNELIA MÜLLER / JAN WEHBERG IN LÜTZOW 7

STORYBOARD

Projects directed by Cornelia Müller and Jan Wehberg: under the name "Lützow 7" the landscape architects design gardens and parks like film sequences. Their directorial role is to make the scene and the protagonists overlap in space in such a way that each place becomes a momentous location, in that it has its own story to tell. The garden or landscape is not merely seen as scenery, it becomes a stage. Landscape, whether it is in the background, the middle ground or the foreground, always relates to the viewer as well as to the actor.

Cornelia Müller and Jan Wehberg define their concept of landscape with reference to Jean François Poussé: "Landscape begins at the point to which feet and eyes are directed. It ends well beyond this, in time and space: it includes gardens and wide sceneries, plants and rocks, towns and derelict land, fields and suburbs. A whole range of opportunities, a whole range of questions that architecture and society have to address. Theory and practice find a broad field to work on here, given increased awareness of the environment. Landscape is always a cultural heritage as well, and one that is shared by many people. It arouses interest precisely for this reason. Creative workers as well as practitioners try to avoid falling into cultural clichés or losing a sense of memory, so that they can give due weight to every dimension, every possible perception."

227
Parking lots, Kirchsteigfeld residential development area, Potsdam, Germany.

228
Detail of the "bastion", Karow-Nord residential development area, Berlin, Germany.

229
Detail at State Insurance Company, Berlin.

230
Deutsches Institut für Normung, Berlin, the German Standards Institute (in MKW with R. Weller). At the centre of the garden court is a fountain in the proportions of a DIN standard page. A historical sequence of characters stands for civilized communication since ancient times.

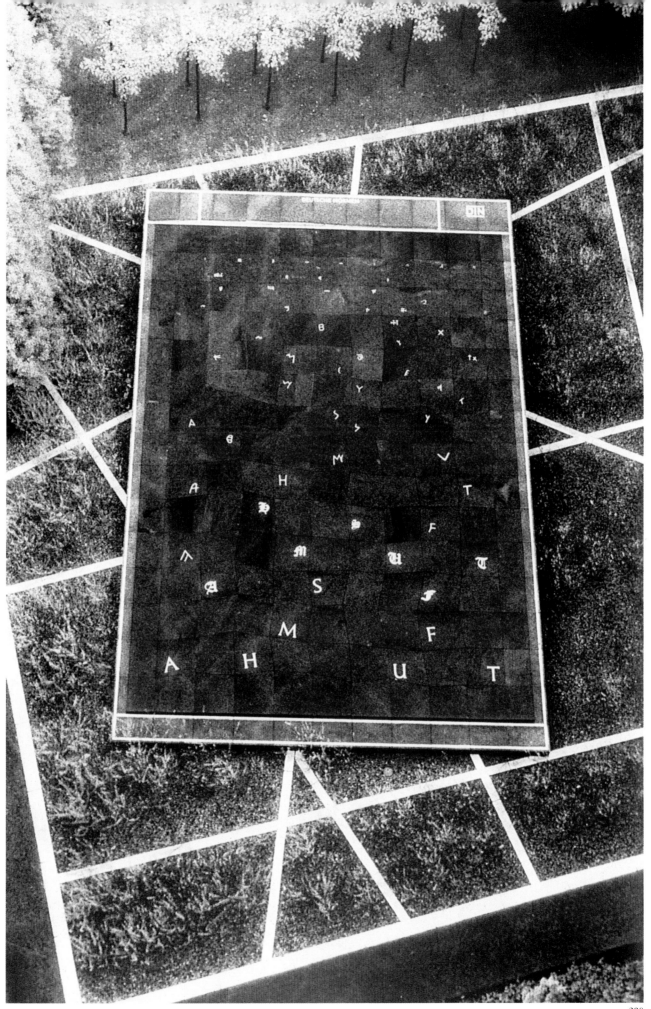

CORNELIA MÜLLER / JAN WEHBERG

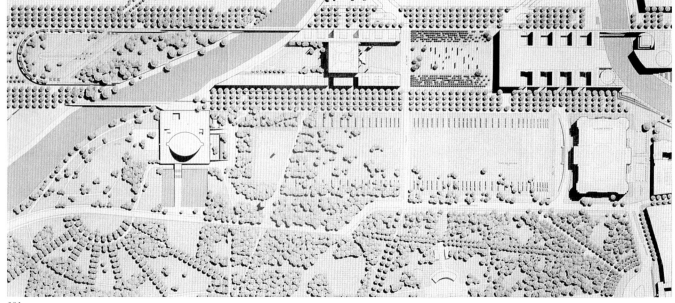

231

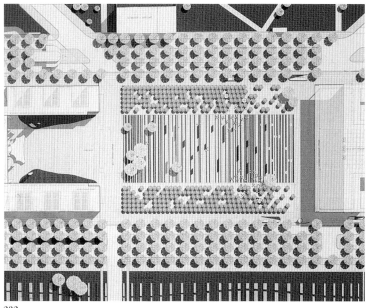

232

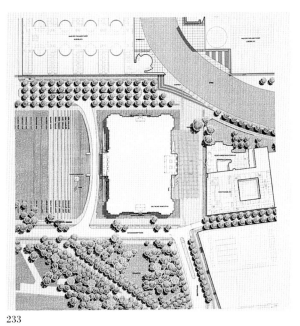

233

231

"Spreebogen" (Spree Bend), Berlin. The new government quarter follows a track-shaped pattern. The open space planning frames the northern edge of the buildings with austere avenues and forms a link with the adjacent Tiergarten park via a prestigious area of lawns with increasingly dense groups of trees.

232

The "Bürgerforum" (Citizen's Forum) is adjacent to the main courtyard of the Chancellery. Temporary water walls, informal groups of trees and two glazed pavilions with kiosk and café organize the space on the users' scale.

233

Ebertplatz, Berlin. A stone carpet of two-by-two-metre granite slabs forms the eastern access to the Reichstag.

234

Due weight for every possible perception? How can landscape be designed on this basis, expressing your own perceptions as a landscape architect by designing space? Cornelia Müller and Jan Wehberg do not want to force their own perceptions on to others: "We believe in interpretation. We do not design à la Müller/Wehberg, but address every job afresh. We want to make people curious. To make effects, but at a second glance. We feel committed to the tradition of garden art. But a style of our own, always using the same resources? Not for us. Our work relates to situations and projects." They reject the attribution of any specific style, but they find "Neue Sachlichkeit" – New Objectivity – quite appropriate: both Modernism and traditionalism are sources from which Müller and Wehberg create new things.

New things should above all relate to the place, be appropriate. This includes going back to horticultural concepts: "Discussion in garden and landscape architecture is still largely driven by questions of participation, of use and care, time and ecology. But we have to go back to the lost content of the discipline, adopt sensual rules for design again and remove the false contrast between aesthetics and use of garden art or landscape design." And yet reintroducing the concept of garden art "should not detract from the merits of ecological approaches or citizens' participation."

234
*"Flying" granite blocks frame the square
and emphasize its horizontal quality vis-
à-vis the façade of the building.*

235

235
Jewish Museum, Berlin (in MKW). A little forest of false acacias, spontaneous vegetation on war rubble, reverses the notion of paradise: wilderness as a paradise on earth as the garden of civilization. A fountain in the form of a sculpted snake runs through the garden as a mythological motif.

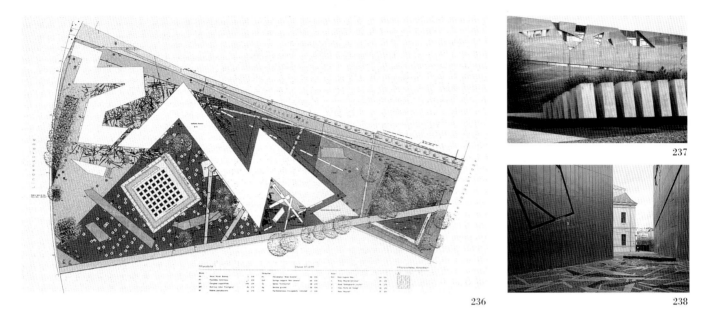

237

236

238

These ecological and participatory elements are inherent in Cornelia Müller's and Jan Wehberg's work, but they do not show on the surface. They say that the only important thing is to find the best for a particular place. "We want to narrate a place's history, and also to tell stories about it. And so we are interested in what substantiates each individual place, how it is grasped or named in terms of space, function or language, in other words how it is defined."

"What are German standards in fact? We looked at drawing up DIN standards and the development of standards in general for DIN's – the German Standards Institute's – garden, until we understood the nature of standardization. That is how the form of the garden now is."

Lützow 7's designs are produced in close co-operation with clients and architects, which finds Müller and Wehberg working with architects as diverse as Axel Schultes (including the German Federal Chancellery, Berlin) and Daniel Libeskind (Jewish Museum, Berlin and Felix Nußbaum Museum, Osnabrück). Their work does not blindly conform with the architect's expressive mode, but does respect it. "For us, the history of garden art offers a whole arsenal of clear forms and compositional rules – in a hierarchy in terms of both time and geography – that have to be rediscovered and developed from today's point of view. Looking backwards shows above all: natural beauty and design interventions are not irreconcilable contrasts. But we seem to have completely forgotten that horticulture is part of our cultural history. Italian Renaissance and Baroque gardens

236
Site plan of the garden of the Jewish Museum, Berlin.

237
The E.T.A. Hoffmann Garden is made up of 7 x 7 columns with oleasters growing in them. The sloping surface is intended to convey a sense of the unstable situation that forced many Jews into the uncertainly of exile.

238
The cramped quality of the Paul Celan Courtyard is reminiscent of a typical Berlin back yard. The pavement pattern is based on a drawing by Paul Celan's wife Gisèle Lestrange Celan.

CORNELIA MÜLLER / JAN WEHBERG

are visually completely different from landscape gardens in Victorian England. There are clear forms and design rules that fit together to form a chain of tradition, a history of styles."

Formal, minimized design elements and their materials are central to the ambition of tying contemporary design into the history of styles. Lützow 7 want to promote a new objectivity with their work, appropriate to the social context of the present day. "It is only this kind of understanding of the elements of a design, and not of a grandiose image, that makes a piece of work, a garden or park, stand out positively in the complex métier of open space planning."

Their unassuming approach applies particularly to public space. "Public space in particular requires aesthetic discipline and carefully considered concepts, that take into account spatial and historical *donnés*, the story of the place, and leave enough space for aspects of ecology and use, so that the idea is still recognizable and convincing in a hundred years' time. Garden planning that intends to do justice to these requirements cannot do without formal consistency. The aesthetic concept that garden and landscape architects develop through abstraction must not be muddied by opportunistic conformism, must not be watered down by changes in detail. Diversity of detail is the simplicity of the whole."

Aiming for simplicity using the resources of garden art is a particular challenge. This is above all due to the nature of plants, which insist on growing and changing all the time. But Müller and Wehberg say: "Gardens must not be afraid of plants." Even if using plants is demanding. "While a building can be illustrated without undue difficulty, appropriately and in a way that enables viewers to imagine it, in the form of a drawing or model, garden plans are more difficult to read. It is difficult to represent living material with compass and ruler, material that is subject to constant change after realization. For this reason, compelling form and informal depth are essential to our planning. It is only with both in place, compelling form and spontaneous, unplanned penetration of spaces that we have a chance of controlling a concept in the long term and of building ourselves into the city's urban and architectural context."

Lützow 7's urban context is above all Berlin. "It is only commitment on the spot that makes the necessary intense planning possible. Being on the spot is a quality that influences every design." But for Müller and Wehberg, being present on the spot, taking part in the discussion process does not mean endlessly arguing and complaining. Who still needs public space? This is one popular discussion subject that landscape architects have foisted on them by their architectural and urban

239
Virtual lines of reference link the architecture with places of Jewish culture in the city. They appear in the external areas as faults in natural stone or railway lines.

240
Felix Nußbaum Museum in Osnabrück, Germany (in MKW): "Das Versteck" (The Hiding-Place) adapts the motif of the artefact from the painter Felix Nußbaum's pictures.

240

241

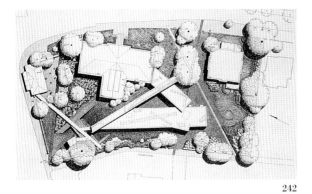

242

243

241
Felix Nußbaum: "Self-Portrait with Apple Blossom", oil on canvas, 1939. The design of the garden draws on associations with the life and work of Felix Nußbaum.

242
Gardens at the Felix Nußbaum Museum. Daniel Libeskind's new building is attached to an old villa.

243
A historical bridge was found on the site and integrated into the overall concept of the garden.

244

245

246

244
State Insurance Company, Berlin (in MKW). A pool of water and a dense grid of plane trees are reminiscent of Islamic models in their calm, geometrical arrangement.

245 | 246
Formal austerity dominates the design, which is fundamentally driven by the function of being a prestigious place that is open to the public.

247

design colleagues. Lützow 7 take a stand: "Horticulture does not have a user problem. It is not there to make individual dreams come true, but to offer something to the public as a whole; use then comes about of its own accord. There is also no conflict between aesthetics and ecology: ecological aspects are in the planning process from the outset, and will be built into a good concept as a matter of course, just like the guidelines laid down by other planners and experts involved. As garden architects, we have to address changes in the architectural argument constantly and constructively. We have to insist on the principle of beauty, and must not give in to conformity. The art of garden design is the art of urban design, which can only be accepted or rejected as a whole. Participation, ecology and use are serving 'sciences' here." Sciences serving the craft of horticulture. Müller and Wehberg do not want to be seen as artists. "We cannot do everything ourselves. For this reason we commit ourselves to what we can do: garden art. Artists are then invited to join in with the design process."

247
Federal Press Association, Berlin. A
water pool surrounds the covered atrium.
Highly artificial lenses made of stone and
(illuminated) glass remind the visitor of
floral elements.

248

249

Lützow 7 are aware that garden art has always been about intelligible symbols. "Understandig the meanings of symbols, which is taken for granted elsewhere, is often rejected as asking too much in Germany. But there has never been a society that has managed without symbols. If the old symbols are no longer valid, then we have to find new ones. Refusing new symbols will only keep old, traditional false ones alive. This does not just apply to architecture, it applies to garden art as well. It is easier for citizens to overlook built architecture that seems alien to them. But parks, landscape gardens, prestigious green areas in cities and public squares arouse their expectations, and so today they need magic again, and a formal language that also admits new symbols."

This courage to embrace the symbolic and at the same time avoiding modish declarations has made Cornelia Müller and Jan Wehberg garden and landscape architects who are able to make convincing statements about historically complicated places like the garden for the Jewish Museum in Berlin or the Platz der Republik outside the Reichstag. Their landscape architecture admits history entirely as a matter of course, but without relying on the past.

248
Federal Ministry of Labour and Social Affairs, Berlin: interior courtyard.

249
Federal Ministry of Economics and Technology, Berlin: interior courtyard.

CORNELIA MÜLLER, born 1952, studied landscape architecture first in Osnabrück and then in Berlin. After winning several competitions, she founded a planning office with Jan Wehberg and Elmar Knippschild in 1979. Since 1997 Cornelia Müller and Jan Wehberg have worked as a duo in "Lützow 7".

JAN WEHBERG, born 1952, studied landscape architecture in Berlin. After successful participation in the Müller, Knippschild, Wehberg (MKW) practice, he has worked as a duo with Cornelia Müller under the name "Lützow 7" since 1997.

Lützow 7 employs fifteen full-time engineers and other staff. The most important projects and competitions started in 1987 with the first prize for the IBA Berlin Tegel harbour project. Müller and Wehberg's realized designs since then include the external area of the extension to the DIN-Institut, Berlin (in MKW, 1993), the State Insurance Company Berlin (in MKW, 1995), the Hotel Bleibtreustraße, Berlin (in MKW, 1995). In 1997 Lützow 7 won the international landscape planning competition "Spreebogen" (Spree Bend) in Berlin. Ebertplatz by the Reichstag was completed in 1999, the Platz der Republik, Forum and Chancellery are to follow. In 1999 the garden for the Jewish Museum in Berlin was completed, designed by Cornelia Müller and Jan Weberg (in MKW) with Daniel Libeskind. The garden for the Felix Nußbaum Museum, Osnabrück (1998) was realised at about the same time. In 2000 Lützow 7 won, among other projects, an international competition for the spa park in Merano, the Rheinpark Neuss, the neighbourhood park Plagwitz/Leipzig, the Garden of the Neandertal Museum and the Berlin-Spandau railway station square.

250

251

252

CORNELIA MÜLLER / JAN WEHBERG

250
Hotel Bleibtreu, Berlin.

251
Playground, Karow-Nord residential area, Berlin.

252
Canal system, Britzer Straße residential complex, Berlin.

SIGHT TAKES THE STAGE

Stefan Rotzler and Matthias Krebs create stage sets. How do visitors to a horticultural show in China imagine a Swiss garden? Rotzler Krebs work on this idea, and not on real Switzerland, in their contribution to the World Horticultural Show in Kunming, China. They play with the images that the Chinese have of Switzerland, and translate these images into a garden vision in stone, plants, water and ice, enrich it with postcard-like photo-walls and fragments of text from Schiller's *William Tell.*

These Swiss architects are interested in teasing a meaning out of landscape, creating the relationship between image and reality. Their key question for every job is how a thing can be given a name and be depicted. "How do we behave towards images as landscape architects? What images do we create?" They used this idea of producing images when staging part of the "Weg der Schweiz" (Swiss Way), which was created in 1991 as a tourist attraction for the 700th anniversary of the Confederate Island. Every canton was allotted an appropriate part of the path to design, so that people could experience the rich diversity of the Swiss landscape. "Walk- and admir-able", as Stefan Rotzler points out. Rotzler Krebs created an image of Switzerland along their part of the path as a sequence of "home" landscapes, gently framed and put into the picture through interventions by the landscape architects, and inviting walkers to stop and look around. The climb up to a viewing platform above the Urnersee was made into a colour journey from blue to white – by using a series of flags, for example.

Rotzler Krebs do not devise clichés, they work with clichés. They are not afraid of visitors' established ideas and expectations, nor do they mind exaggerating things, and so they produce impressive, powerful designs that lose none of their charisma when realized. And it is the most sensitive of these works that produce images of particular intensity, rather than reticence. Pink flowering cherries were planted in front of a reddish-coloured concrete wall for the courtyard of the parish centre in Winterthur. The resulting image positively leaps at the viewer – and sticks in the memory. Especially as Rotzler Krebs balance their design with almost effortless ease by using small cobblestones, concrete steps and a "water table", a long reflecting pool in black concrete, in the ensemble of the courtyard.

253   254   255

Their courtyards, parks and gardens all show lucidity of design paired with effortlessly deployed elements, some of which are quite fanciful. The landscape architects' understanding of the material used in each case makes the gardens clearly intelligible, because they show individual handwriting. At the same time the sensitive choice of materials completely avoids slipping away into kitsch.

Rotzler Krebs's vision of gardens is internationally trained. The courtyard design for a commercial building in Opfikon shows Japanese influence, and they chose Mediterranean elements for the park of a rehabilitation clinic – though these were severely reduced and placed in a clear frame. Rotzler Krebs do not cultivate exuberant gardens and the image that goes with them. "No excess caused by plant growth. Instead of this, composed plant-pictures, that push aspects like yellow blossom or lancet leaves into the foreground", as Matthias Krebs explains. The criterion of a precisely defined level of intensity in an image is also applied as a yardstick for the international garden quotations they use, though strictly speaking these are not quotations. On the contrary, they are inspirations that were allowed to shape the approach in a specific design, beautifully controlled by the staging landscape architects.

It is easy to see that it is delight in images that motivates Rotzler Krebs's work, and delight in playing with images. They created enormous "insects" made of trimmed box and metal bows as a repeated and thus uniquely powerful element for the courtyard of an insurance firm's offices.

253
Building-high photographic prints formed the backdrop for the Swiss garden at the World Horticulture Show in Kunming, China.

254
Visitors could experience the gardens as a theatrical event from barrel-like boats on the "Schifflibach".

255
The idea of the garden is to make people happy and curious, rather than merely conveying "information". The main attraction of the garden in subtropical Kunming was the refreshingly cool ice grotto.

256

257

The "insects" are freely distributed all over the courtyard and appear to be wading through water, crowding together to protect the terrace that has been opened for employees or just lying in the sun.

Much work from the Rotzler Krebs office shows the pleasure that the designers take in looking for ideas and associations. The "dancing ellipses", an art installation at Zurich airport, realized in 1991, offered approaching people and planes a puzzle picture that plays with perception and with disturbing this perception. The eye looking down from the air looks for an order, a system, but ultimately remains captured simply by the sequence of images resulting from the speed at which the viewer is travelling. Moving pictures are created in the heads of moving viewers.

The "Swiss Garden" (with Anarchitekten, Switzerland) shown at the International Horticultural Show in Kunming, China, in 1999 offered every possible image and association that Asia could come up with on the subject of Switzerland: mountains, snow, mountain stream. Snow was made

256
Courtyard to a parish centre in Winterthur, Switzerland. A narrow viewing slit creates links between the interior and the exterior. The quiet surface of the long, dark-coloured water table reflects the twilight of the roof of leaves and the sky. On the courtyard side the water falls over a rough wall surface and fills the room with sounds.

257
A run of red-coloured wall marks the boundary with the street.

258
Courtyard of the "Galleria" building in Opfikon, Switzerland: Plant troughs raise the bands of vegetation into the third dimension. Japanese maple is used to establish the atmosphere.

259
The narrow space is dramatized by additional separation. The main accent is provided by a pierced longitudinal wall built of massive sandstone slabs that divides the space.

258

259

260

261

262

260
*Headquarters of an insurance company,
Zurich, Switzerland: four linked sections
of the courtyard are brought together by
the insect-like topiary motif.*

261
*Three sets of evergreen plants create a
sense of fluent space in the cafeteria
courtyard and yet give a sense of distance
between the directors' canteen and the
staff restaurant.*

262
*The narrow space of the reception court-
yard is further stressed by designed emptiness. A water-mirror projects the play of
the clouds into the adjacent rooms.*

263

264

265

263
*Design for the external areas of a rehabil-
itation clinic in Bellikon, Switzerland:
zones of urban frugality, of horticultural
luxuriance . . .*

264
*. . . of diversity that is close to nature, of
Romantic playfulness come together to
form a very varied complex. The planning
scheme also addresses therapeutic
requirements, for walking practice, for
instance.*

265
*Social security offices for the canton of
Zurich: Long ribbon hedges in the shade
of an avenue of pagoda trees reflect the
horizontal façade structure of the office
building and create a link with the front
gardens that are a feature of the district.*

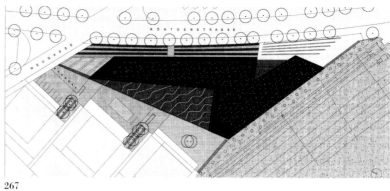

266

267

artificially, different heights were created with metal frameworks, the mountain world was shown as a photographic panorama. Delighted visitors raced down the stylized mountain stream in wooden barrels. A garden? A joke.

This is a game with clichés, not kitsch. Eloquent design that has a lot to say to us and about which a lot can be said, but not "design loquacity", against which the author and landscape architect Udo Weilacher issues urgent warnings. Other nations' contributions to the International Horticultural Show in China show how difficult it can be to walk this tightrope. For example, the Austrian contribution consisted of a piece of floral border from a park in the capital, Vienna, which was simply copied in China – complete with a golden bust of Johann Strauss in the middle of the bed. It was Rotzler who – when visiting Vienna – pointed this banality out to the assembled landscape architects by showing a photograph of this flowerbed after a slide show on his own projects. A lot of people find this direct approach arrogant. Rotzler comes back: "We work on the basis of a radical perception – a truth assessment – of what is there. We decode situations and problems and develop succinct images from them. Perhaps the provocative element of these images lies in an uncompromising combination of things and themes that superficially have little to do with each other. This releases energy in viewers. Creates aggression, joy, excitement, laughter."

This self-confidence makes Rotzler Krebs open to gestures that are as impressive as they are considered. These landscape architects stage gardens, and so they are operating close to fine art, but also to film and theatre. Garden stages. They take their public seriously by entertaining them in the best sense of the word: without any fuss, and with a great deal of expertise and wit. Rotzler Krebs stand for aggressive and yet sensitive self-assertion of landscape architecture in the world of media and goods. They know that in a multi-media society our aesthetic understanding, our ability to make pictures, did not come to a standstill with the landscape garden. For this reason the "Augen-weide" (Feast/Pasture for the Eye) alludes brilliantly to the age of media aesthetics. The "Augenweide" was conceived for the Potsdam "Feldflur", or community farmland, for a landscape that was originally designed by Peter Joseph Lenné (1789–1866). Rotzler Krebs here cooperated with Otmar Sattel, Berlin and an agricultural engineer. "Who or what defines a landscape? Are there protagonists? As far as we are concerned, it is not the spirit of Lenné that hovers above this land in Potsdam. And anyway, Lenné is taken far too seriously. It is the cattle that make farmland into a living landscape – and they play the lead in our script for a temporary staging of the Potsdam Feldflur." Rotzler Krebs defined their project as "Lenné with a wink". And they do not ask any more questions about the way Lenné, the garden artist, looks at things, but how the cow sees them: how does a cow actually see landscape? Colourful pasture fences give a structure to the area in an unspectacular layout. Herds of farm animals remind us of peasant agriculture. The Berlin artist Otmar Sattel developed so-called "video horns" for some of the cows: miniature cameras attached to the cow's horns show things from the animal's point of view, and the ensuing images of landscape are shown on monitors. This piece of landscape art is to be shown as a temporary staging in Potsdam in 2001. Rotzler Krebs Partner will then be offering a further contribution to cultivated vision, an up-to-date and entertaining lesson on landscape architecture as staged sight.

268

266
A roof garden that can be looked into, laid out as a dynamic garden image. Strips of grass that are constantly blown about by the wind create changing perspectives.

267
The new building forms an urban periphery on the edge of an open area of railway lines. A transformed "rail garden" is staged on the railway side, with steel tubes planted in parts. Groups of oak trees with multiple gnarled trunks create an intermediate zone.

268
Repetitive surface lines, ball-lamps placed in the open space: the design for the entrance to the FIFA headquarters in Zurich takes up images and associations with football in a light-hearted way.

269

270

271

272

269 | 270 | 271 | 272
"Dancing ellipses": an "aerial picture"
for passengers coming into land was
staged at Zurich's Kloten airport on the
occasion of the 700th anniversary of
Switzerland, "CH-91".

21

STEFAN ROTZLER, born 1953, has worked with MATTHIAS KREBS, born 1965, since 1989. Rotzler Krebs have offices in Winterthur and Gockhausen (Zurich). They employ six staff at the time of writing. Stefan Rotzler has taught on various occasions at the Hochschule Rapperswil and at the ETH Zürich.

Rotzler Krebs' most important projects include the Swiss Garden at the International Horticultural Exhibition, Kunming (People's Republic of China) 1999 and the "Augenweide" project, Bornstedter Feldflur, in Potsdam (BUGA 2001), which they have been working on since 1998. The office was responsible for the overall concept and the Canton of Zurich's section of the "Weg der Schweiz" by the Urnersee from 1984–91. The Neuwiesen, Winterthur courtyard design dates from 1992–94. From 1990–95, Rotzler Krebs designed and realized the outdoor facilities for the "Rheinstahlstraße" residential development for the Prosper-Park in Bottrop for IBA Emscher Park. The office worked on landscaping the grounds of the SUVA rehabilitation clinic in Bellikon from

1991–99. The outdoor facilities for the SVA offices in Zurich and the "Schönaustraße" residential development in Basel date from 1997–99. Landscape concepts by Rotzler Krebs provided important principles and stimuli for urban development in Lyon ("Plaine de l'Est"), for expansion to the north of Tel Aviv ("Pi Glilot"), and form the basis for urban development in the Zug region of Switzerland.

At the time of writing the office is planning the Hilti headquarters in Schaan, Liechtenstein, the municipals gardens in Dornbirn, Austria, the "International Primary School" in Wädenswil, Switzerland, and various public parks, large residential developments and private gardens.

273

ROTZLER KREBS PARTNER

273

The "Augenweide" (Feast/Pasture for the Eye) will be in place during the Federal Horticultural Show in Potsdam, Germany in 2001. Facets of pastoral farming and the way in which it is perceived are trans *formed artistically. Grazing cows wear video cameras on their horns. Visitors can experience what the cows are seeing – an everyday artistic and artificial landscape.*

A CHANGE OF SCENERY

GROSS. MAX. is Bridget Baines, Eelco Hooftman and Ross Ballard. They are landscape architects who like to talk straight. Their designs and explanations are as open as they are lucid. They prefer to write the explanations of their designs with all the conciseness and profundity of an essay, often in a peculiar auto-interview format. GROSS. MAX. understands that finding the right answer means asking the right question in the first place. They are passionate about confronting the public and proclaiming ideas in the form of images or words. And their answers are as comprehensive as they are provocative. Often too provocative for a public that looks for peace of mind in gardens and landscape. GROSS. MAX. does not offer relief, but something to chew on, mentally.

GROSS. MAX. declares historical heritage to be "architectural necrophilia", complaining that "ecological megalomania is "regressive striving for a rural idyll" and demands a "Pandora's box full of metropolitan sensual delights". "Why suffocate in an overdose of chlorophyll if we can boost our level of adrenaline instead? Parks should not spread over cities like a green stain; on the contrary, they should be confined to special designated sanctuaries; the park as a hunting-ground for the contemporary citizens." The city is seen as an event, the park as a cultural and traditional domain for hedonistic pleasure. And this is not all about horticultural extravaganzas but about new approaches to defining public spaces. "We like the simple notion of 'a change of scenery'; it reveals a basic desire for exotic holiday destinations, compulsive adultery and most important it provides the rationale behind most landscape projects."

Are gardens, parks and landscapes suitable testing grounds for new ideas? Eelco Hooftman followed this theme through the history of garden art in a research project called "The Avant-Garden: The Garden as Manifesto". The result: gardens are traditionally test-beds for the future. And so GROSS. MAX. started experimenting. The ideas behind their designs, presentations and explanations constantly attempt to capture a project's location and requirements as comprehensively as possible in the past and the present, so that they can plumb the possibilities for future development. For this development GROSS. MAX. put forward suggestions that are as imaginative as they are far-reaching on the plane of an avant-garde perception of culture – they refer to "avant-gardens as antibodies in the metropolitan blood stream".

274

275

276

274
Whiteinch Cross: this design for an urban square in Glasgow was produced in 1999 as part of the "UK City of Architecture and Design" programme.

275
The square is structured by two free-standing walls and a transparent pergola construction in galvanized steel. The walls are clad with Corten steel, a material that takes up Glasgow's tradition of steel-making and ship-building.

276
The square is divided into two levels. The higher platform is laid with yellow sand-stone slabs, whose iron oxide deposits provide a rust-red banding effect.

277

278

277
Water pours down one of the Corten steel walls along a length of eight metres. This curtain of water is lit from below at night.

278
A twelve-metre-high concrete column marks the road junction. The colour of the Corten steel varies with the weather, from dark rust when it is raining to glowing orange on sunny days.

279 | 280
The concrete column exudes a blue light that varies in colour according to climatic changes in the air.

279   280

This delight in experiments quickly attracted attention: competition wins in Hanover for EXPO 2000 ("Hangover EXPO 2001") and repeatedly in Berlin, contributions to Glasgow City of Architecture & Design 1999, and also their first realized projects.

Their optimism about the future is like a breath of fresh air in British landscape architecture, which remains largely conservative. GROSS. MAX. juxtaposes contemporary landscape architecture in Britain with its magnificent history, which they want to link up with in terms of ambition, rather than in any formal sense: "During the seventeenth and eighteenth centuries, Great Britain was the testing ground for many experiments in landscape architecture. Landscape was a topic of intensive aesthetic discourse and philosophical enquiry. The essence of British Landscape Architecture was to reshape nature according to fashion and taste – the cult of the cultivar, the art of the artefact. Landscape was the domain of dandies, hermits, painters and poets. In comparison the twentieth century produced work of little or no interest."

In this search for a new authenticity for landscape, its various layers are to be peeled off and disentangled – "not unlike the seductive act of striptease". "The landscape architect should combine the seductiveness of Mata Hari with the shrewdness of Miss Marple. The very concept of landscape is based on visual pleasure. From seventeenth century Claude Lorrain glasses to twentieth century camcorders we screen the landscape through the eyes of a voyeur. Scenery and scenario are the

Siamese twins of landscape – from the garden of Epicures to the garden of Eurotrash. In the visual jungle of contemporary society the citizen hunts, not to survive but for sheer pleasure; like the cat tossing the mouse into the air. The ultimate destination of landscape is to become a hedonistic pleasure zone. Landscape should be convulsive or should not be at all."

GROSS. MAX. is frequently keen to draw attention to their ideas by entering international competitions or participating in design workshops. For example with their design for the banks of the River Clyde in Glasgow as a "Blue Light District": "Cranes lift purpose-designed porta-Kabins which can be rented on an hourly basis. The various cabins would swing in the sky, float on the water or even be sunk underneath the water surface. They provide a unique stage set for business meetings, wedding anniversaries or an amorous rendezvous. Aviaries with canaries provide the soundtrack of everlasting spring. […] The river is illuminated with blue underwater lights. A so-called 'Body Building', a glazed high-rise dedicated to fitness, will act as a new landmark next to Central Station."

GROSS. MAX. was similarly provocative with their design for EXPO 2000 in Hanover. A large part of the site remained a cornfield. "We did not design the cornfield, we simply left it there. The field suddenly becomes a foreign body when surrounded by EXPO; an objet trouvé of surrealistic design. But not as an illusion, as a reality. This is a productive field that changes colour with the season: from an innocent light green to a riot of golden yellow. The lonely farmer on his combine harvester becomes a hedonistic hero of EXPO 2000. The harvest, the ploughing of the field, all this becomes a show event as part of the exhibition. Ultimately designing a World Fair is like organizing a party. The pavilions are 'guests of honour' at an architectural fancy-dress party. Some will certainly behave badly and attract attention to themselves, others sit still in their corners like the

281

282

283

281
Sandveien: a 70s estate in Lerwick, Shetland, Great Britain was given a new sense of articulation by elegantly curved dry-stone walls. Public and private areas are clearly separated here.

282 | 283
The walls are a re-interpretation of so-called "plantiecrubs": a traditional way of cultivating vegetable in small enclosures in which a special microclimate is created.

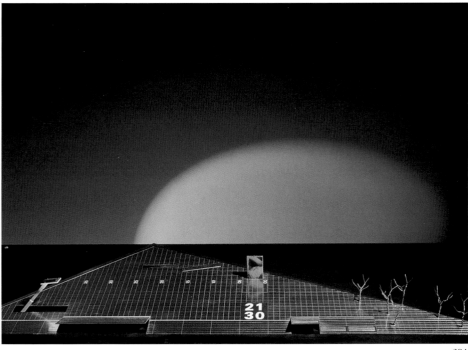
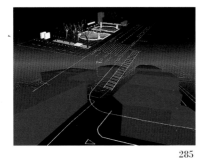

284

285

eternal wallflower. A party requires constant improvisation, like a play without a script. Organized anarchy." But GROSS. MAX. does not just give landscape its head, they think about the consequences: "A party like a World Fair is transient by definition. It leaves marks on the carpet, glasses and relationships are broken. The fundamental dilemma of EXPO 2000 in Hanover is how you organize a party without waking up with a hangover the next morning – Hangover EXPO 2001."

Landscape architecture and a refusal to plan are not mutually exclusive for this approach. But there are no ecological arguments that can be mustered in favour of this, but conceptual considerations about the relationship between development in time and space. "Ecology is not the object of our desire", GROSS. MAX. proclaim, and in their competition entry for the Falkenberg Estate in Berlin plant nothing but botanical exotics outside the door for the Germans, who are obsessed with the idea of preserving native – 'natural' – vegetation. "We constantly question the boundaries between what is seen as 'natural' and what as 'artificial'." But at the same time they suggest a "Five Year Non-Plan" for parts of the area. They agreed that the time had come for the exhibition, but not the time for implementing plans in this peripheral place.

284
Potsdamer Platz, Berlin, Germany. 1995 competition entry. "We love the wonderful German word Lustgarten. We dream of a kind of urban striptease in which the various layers are peeled off slowly and sensuously. Peepholes allow glimpses into the depths of the various rail and road tunnels, while periscopes are installed in the underground station so that people can look at the world above them."

285
Hackney Town Hall Square, London, Great Britain: historical maps show that there used to be a grove on the site of the present main square in the London district of Hackney. The idea of a grove of flowering trees combined with an essentially urban area is the basis of the design's duality.

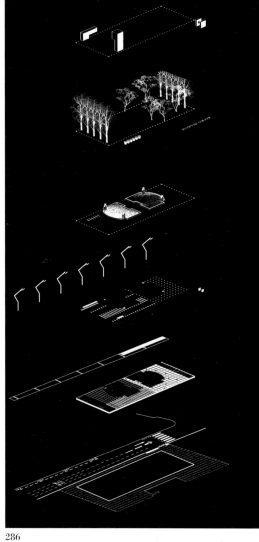

286

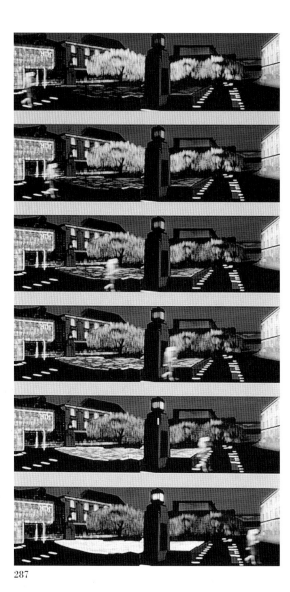

287

288

286
Two simple but impressive new structures make a communicative interface for the urban public: a bus-stop that is also an information panel and a public gallery for local artists, and a kiosk with a video wall. The surface of the square is treated as a carpet, on which the three-dimensional design elements are placed.

287
The square is conceived as an interactive composition. A sound system that responds to people's movements is built into the surface covering. The brightness and colour of the under-water illumination are computer-controlled. A "weather strip" with smoke machine, water jets, wind machine and hot air and a light installation in the square complete the design.

288
The square becomes an open-air foyer for the adjacent public and cultural buildings. Former flowerbeds will be turned into pools of water. Miniature boats can be hired from a "square warden" at the kiosk.

The first built project by these Edinburgh based landscape architects was on the remote Shetland Islands. GROSS. MAX. has come a long way out of this "splendid isolation", all the way to their recent success in London. Whiteinch Cross built in Glasgow 1998/99 provided an important stepping stone. A lot of fresh starts happened to be in the air at the same time, leading to some concrete opportunities – for the city and for Great Britain's long tradition of landscape architecture, a country that still has world-famous gardens and parks but has done little to address public spaces in today's cities.

Glasgow has faced up to the trend for rediscovering public space and declared itself "UK City of Architecture and Design" in 1999. The "5–Spaces" project was launched as a response to good experience in Barcelona and other cities with investment in public space: five neglected sites in Glasgow were developed into new and exciting public spaces for the local communities. The creation and artistic highlighting of public spaces produced new initiatives, including local neighbourhood projects and job creation initiatives.

Given its creative responsibility for the Whiteinch Cross project, the practice was now confronted with the necessary attention to detail. The result is convincing. And yet GROSS. MAX. continue to be pleased to be thought of as "funky". They quickly set a new course by combining a delight in provocation that had been tried and tested in Europe with planning sensitivity tried and tested in Scotland for a competition for Hackney Town Hall Square in London in 1999. Result: they won the competition. The assertion is now that "Delirious Hackney will become the epicentre of London's urban transformation". If this comes off, GROSS. MAX. will become the epicentre of transformation – and not just for British landscape architecture: a little earthquake.

289
Centre for Contemporary Art and the Natural World, Exeter, Great Britain: "The Walled Garden".

GROSS. MAX.

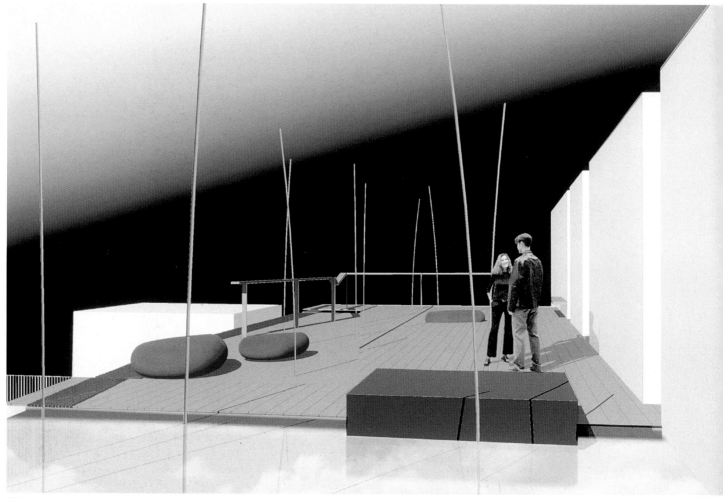

290

291

290
Roof garden for an office building in Edinburgh, Great Britain: a sky-mirror, aerials and red seating make a living landscape above the city that is familiar and alienated at the same time.

291
St John's Square, London: Lighting as a cheap material providing great effects.

292
The "Earth Centre" in Doncaster, Great Britain, on the site of a former coal-mine, was funded by the Royal Scottish Academy.

292

293   294

BRIDGET BAINES, born 1958, and EELCO HOOFTMAN, born 1960, founded GROSS. MAX. in 1995. ROSS BALLARD, born 1974, joined in 1999. Bridget Baines studied landscape architecture at Heriot-Watt University / Edinburgh School of Art. During the 1990's Bridget Baines taught landscape Architecture at Edinburgh School of Art and was visiting lecturer in Denmark, France, Italy and Japan.

Eelco Hooftman worked in a travelling circus before studying landscape architecture at the Agricultural University of Wageningen. In 1990 he became Design Tutor at the Edinburgh College of Art. Hooftman has been guest lecturer at institutions including the Academie van Bouwkunst in Amsterdam, and in Japan.

GROSS. MAX.' first collaborative scheme was an award winning scheme for Two Parks at Potsdamer Platz in Berlin (Ankauf), soon followed by an award for their landscape master plan for Hannover Expo 2000 (Ankauf). Since the completion of Whiteinch Square as part of Glasgow '99 City of Architecture and Design and the first prize in the RIBA competition for Hackney Town Hall Square the practice has been recognised for its contextual approach with a contemporary idiom towards urban space. Other projects for public space include St John's Square London (first prize limited competition) and Merry Hill Plaza, Birmingham. Examples of the garden as field of experiment include the master plan for The Centre for Contemporary Art and the Natural World at Poltimore House Exeter, the design of a Carboniferous Garden with American artist Mark Dion at the Earth Centre Doncaster, a Hortus Medicus at the new Medical School at Glasgow University and a roof top garden for an office building in Edinburgh.

Collaboration with artists includes Adam Barker-Mill (Whiteinch Cross and Hackney Town Hall Square), Mark Dion (Carboniferous Garden Earth Centre), Garry Fabian-Miller (Poltimore House), Alan Johnston and Matt Rogalsky (Hackney Town Hall Square).

293 | 294
GROSS. MAX. and the artist Mark Dion are designing the "Carboniferous Garden", an artificial marsh landscape that takes us into a primeval world from the age when the coal seams were laid down.

295

WEST 8

STORMY AND SCEPTICAL

Adriaan Geuze is a quiet star. Perfect public appearances, lectures on landscape architecture and also landscape architecture as show business. Geuze has an abundance of ideas, but he is sometimes quite sceptical about his work.

The West 8 office is not just Adriaan Geuze. A team of landscape architects, town planners, architects, designers and botanists works on projects that are aimed at pushing ideas as far as they will go. A "joyously experimental combination of a radical approach to art and landscape architecture and ecological sensitivity" (Udo Weilacher). West 8 announce themselves as "landscape architects & urban planners", with their logo of a full wind-sock – west wind force 8. They devise concepts for the future of towns and the landscape. And West 8 puts these concepts into practice – in urban planning and also as parks or open spaces in the broadest sense of the word. Thus urban districts, squares, gardens and landscapes become text-book examples of professional work.

295
*Borneo/Sporenburg, Amsterdam, The
Netherlands: Two former docks, residential development with a density of 100
units per hectare. Detached houses on a
uniform pattern are interrupted by three
super-blocks.*

296
*The image of a container port was behind
the guidelines that West 8 devised for this
development with 2,400 residential units.*

297
*Sculptural bridges connect the two penin-
sulas.*

296

297

298

299

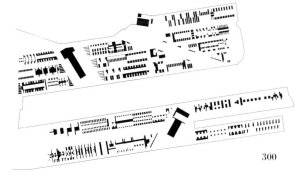

300

298 | 299
Private patios and public space are close-ly connected with each other.

300
Mass plan of private patios and two pub-lic parks.

301

Their most recent urban development project, in Amsterdam harbour, became a built manifesto by West 8. The harbour islands of Borneo and Sporenburg have become a residential area. The City of Amsterdam chose the office's masterplan for realization in 1992. Urban planning for 2 400 homes as a commission for landscape architects? The experiment came off. West 8 developed guidelines that were as austere as they were lucid. A cityscape designed like a landscape painting, although without the Romantic intentions of traditional European landscape painting. But the principle of basing the design on an image remained. While conventional town planning adds functions on, and pays attention to the balance between living area, open space and circulation space, West 8 insisted on the image that Adriaan Geuze and his team had in their heads. It was an image of a harbour, of course, as the history and structure of the site were steeped in its use as a harbour: long shorelines, narrow pieces of land thrusting into the water.

Adriaan Geuze is fond of Dutch history. And yet he was not working on a historical image of a port with masts and rigging, houseboats and reefed sails, but the image of a container port. Adriaan Geuze is fond of Dutch modernity and Modernism.

301
Schouwburgplein, Rotterdam, The Netherlands: The square is raised 35 centimetres above street level and gives the impression of a floating platform. The emptiness of the area stimulates urban activity – a few props are enough.

302
The lighting masts, reminiscent of cranes, change their position at pre-programmed times. But the scenery can also be controlled by passers-by.

303
Neon lighting that reacts to movement interactively is installed under the perforated metal plates that cover the surface of the square. The square asserts its architectural identity at night by outdoing its surroundings, which are also brightly lit.

302

303

304

Living in a container port? The landscape architects did not push it as far as that. West 8 planned their homes as an estate of terraced houses: low rise – high density, a very Dutch approach. In rough contrast to the open and cosmic space of the water, each house has its enclosed patio. This creates a direct dialogue between personal individual Eden and the mighty Dutch sky. It is easier to understand West 8's work if you take a look at Dutch history, which is a history of planning and building. Adriaan Geuze stresses that nature and landscape are traditionally valued and perceived rather differently in the Netherlands than in the rest of Europe. The Netherlands are artificial by nature – "manmade". The epitome of this idea of nature is the polder: land that has been enclosed by dikes and drained, created by engineers and pumps. Geuze's grandfather was a dike construction engineer. And for this reason it was also entirely natural for Geuze to see nature and landscape as artificial.

Most of the homes on Borneo and Sporenburg were complete by the year 2000. Critics are astonished by how consistently the planner managed to make his image into a reality – in association with a number of architects who worked on individual buildings and lines of terraced houses, and on three large-scale forms or super-blocks, which were hurled onto the landscape of terraced houses with scant regard for any order. These conscious acts of aggression were intended as sculptural disturbances. And these disturbances are visibly good for the cityscape, as they help viewers to be much more aware of the contrasting low building, without it being tiring.

304
Garden of a Bank, Utrecht, The Nether-
lands: a prestigious garden with strips
of box trees and sandstone sculpture
is placed below a 90 metre high building.
The reptilian bridge is the way to an
adjacent, ecologically valuable park.

305

306

Geuze wants to design and develop, not to heal and rescue. For him there is no "lost nature". He is suspicious of this romantic motif, which has had such an impact on European landscape architecture. And yet he is not a landscape engineer, but a landscape artist. He is fascinated by the image of the Dutch landscape, with all its breadth, big skies, light and colours. Thus an image can drive the design, in urban development as well.

What influence can the image of a town have on town planning? The urban guidelines derived from the image have penetrated to the very concept of the dwellings on Borneo and Sporenburg. A three-storey development, but the dwellings are not arranged as flats, but as family houses with individual access to the courtyard and the street. There is on-site parking, which in the case of parcels that are only 4.2 metres wide by up to 40 metres deep means integral garages. Fundamentally flat roofs and a "garden", either as a patio yard, a loggia or a roof terrace. These guidelines from Geuze derived from his image, from the general impression that all the architects involved had to accept.

However – Adriaan Geuze's urban dictates were not implemented because the landscape architect's image convinced everybody, but because Geuze could argue his concept through persuasively: families want to (and should) live individually, not on an upper floor, but in touch with the ground. But individuality should not make undue demands: the home-owners did not want gardens of their own, that they would have to cultivate, design and maintain. They would prefer a fully enclosed

305
Interpolis Garden, Tilburg, The Netherlands: water-tables between 20 and 85 metres long, strips of grass and paths laid with bark mulch are placed at odd angles to each other, and offer constantly changing and unusual perspectives. The garden is open to the public during the day and has power points and net access so that employees can work outdoors.

306
Large slabs of slate like roof tiles form a carpet at the foot of the building. Their changes of direction repeat the shifts in the strips of grass.

307

courtyard, private and secret. And Geuze even went a step further. He reduced not mainly the private, but above all public space as much as possible. Open space, with buildings close by all around, is private space on Borneo and Sporenburg. Only the street access is public. This shows conceptual consistency from the West 8 office, which has been criticized as an "inclination to exaggerate", but was rewarded in this case. A piece of city has been created that is much praised and very lively, a prototype for building in a confined space.

The first piece of work that was a popular success for West 8 was also conceptually strong. A gigantic barrier, the largest hydraulic project in Europe, was built at the mouth of the Oosterschelde in the early nineties, as a protection against storm tides. After the barrier was built, it was agreed that some work on landscape architecture should also be part of the project. West 8 put through a concept that did not simply prettify technology by tying it into new landscapes. But the new landscape – man-made, of course – emphasizes the intervention, continues it. "Mussel beds", some laid on a square grid, others in strips, made up of black mussels and white cockles, waste from a nearby mussel farm, offered a new pattern that was intended to attract breeding sea-birds, on the principle of camouflage in the choice of a place for sitting on eggs. An ecologically justified design that placed its hopes in the birds' creativity and at the same time is a work of art telling a story about the everyday nature of landscape – waste shells on land left over from a building-site. But the birds weren't playing.

Previously West 8 had already attracted attention with their design for the Visserijplein in Rotterdam (1990, realized 1995). A simple square that can be used just as easily for a market as for playing street football emerged from a report on the possibilities of upgrading a socially difficult suburb. Robust tree sculptures in stainless steel provide a special feature for the square. The "branches" have power connections for the market stalls built into them – functional elements and

307 | 308

Environment design for Schiphol airport, Amsterdam: in the entrance hall, Holland, the land of tulips, greets the world with colourfully planted troughs of flowers – and the world returns the greeting!

309

The large areas of the airport are clad in a grid of birch trees. As a "green veil" they offer a way of recognizing the airport and tie its disparate components like buildings, infrastructure and information panels together into a coherent whole.

The birch trees' ecological qualities prevent certain larger species of birds – that are dangerous in the airport area because they get caught up in the aircraft engines – from establishing themselves.

a statement at the same time: urban greenery does not help everywhere, sometimes simulation is more useful. "I spend half my time on phone calls", says Adriaan Geuze, "in which I am asked about 'green fingers', 'green lungs', 'green hearts', which are all things we are supposed to deliver as landscape architects. That is our job. But there are correct and incorrect ways of making nature part of the city."

The Schouwburgplein in Rotterdam finally clinched West 8's international reputation. A square defined by three elements only was designed between the municipal theatre and a new cinema, representing nothing more than it actually is: a square. The Schouwburgplein is the epitome of a public, urban location: paving made up of different materials – metal, wood, stone – continues the cinema's material experiment in semi-transparent lightweight façades. The square is slightly higher than the street because there is a car-park under it, and this also makes the Schouwburgplein into something rather special. A custom-designed bench, which takes up the whole length of the square, provides seating for a lot of people and is a good meeting-place if you want to catch up with things. Four gigantic lights in the form of mobile cranes are fun elements and at the same time reminiscent of Rotterdam harbour. Visitors to the square can adjust these cranes themselves, and so constantly affect the design by changing light and form. Everyday, public urban entertainment.

Geuze identifies strongly with the design for the Schouwburgplein. But he is very critical about other landscape architecture designs – even his own. He doubts that there is an ideal of beauty for landscape architecture. "Being hungry to design something beautiful leads to undue tolerance of one's own idea's. And the whole thing is about controlling ideas. It is only by controlling your own ideas that you will produce a beautiful garden." West 8 has built beautiful gardens like this – as a link between buildings and landscape. "And that is all. But it is often a vain attempt." In fact a place only becomes a garden in the viewer's mind.

309

310

310
Typical "non-places" in the transport infrastructure like motorway access roads, multi-storey and underground car-parks were included in the design concept and play with ideas of nature and artificiality like the other areas.

311
Surreal isolation: Adriaan Geuze created a light installation made up of frames and Spanish moss in a cypress marsh near Charleston, USA in 1997 on the occasion of the annual "Spoleto Art Festival".

For this reason, West 8 gave up the idea of designing a landscape when working on the landscaping of Amsterdam's Schiphol airport. "We were simply concerned to initiate a landscape development. We planted hundreds of thousands of birch trees, absolutely everywhere, sowed clover as a fertilizing agent and commissioned a beekeeper to set up beehives. An ecological cycle was established, and everything is getting greener and greener as time goes by. If the trees are in the way we simply dig them up again. Ultimately an airport site like this changes very quickly. Why design a poetic image for a location like this? Sometimes we simply avoid trying to create a design. Then we are just engineers for bioprocesses."

Geuze waits to see what effect his provocation has, and is content – and then he comes up with what is probably his most poetic work so far: Swamp Garden in Charleston, USA.

WEST 8 was founded in Rotterdam in 1987. At the moment ADRIAAN GEUZE manages the office with EDZO BINDELS and HENK HARZEMA. A team of architects, designers, town planners and landscape architects work with them. Geuze studied landscape architecture at the Agricultural University in Wageningen. Today he alternates between teaching jobs, including work at the Delft Polytech in Holland and in Århus, Denmark. Like other West 8 colleagues, Adriaan Geuze is a frequent speaker at international conferences in his field. West 8 won the international Prix de Rome in 1990, the Dutch Maaskant Award for young architects in 1995 and 2000. West 8's work has won numerous international competitions, even though most of their realized projects are in the Netherlands. Geuze's suggestion that there is something special about the Dutch perception of landscape is obviously true.

The most important works and competitions: West 8 designed the Oosterschelde project in 1991, the Schouwburgplein in Rotterdam in 1991–92, which was realized from 1996. Planting at Schiphol airport near Amsterdam occupied West 8 from 1994 to 1996. The urban design masterplan for the harbour islands of Borneo and Sporenburg dates from 1993, and realization continued into 2000.

312

313

314

312
Garden Makeblijde, The Netherlands:
"At first a vertical landscape, a tower of green, a golden blob ...

313
... and then a romantic patio, a contemplative inner sanctuary, with lilies, frogs, a nymph ..."

314
A vertical park that conveys the vision of contemporary landscape architects in 30 individual gardens.

ACKNOWLEDGEMENTS

COVER
Erik-Jan Ouwerkerk

BATLLE I ROIG
Batlle i Roig 11, 14, 16, 17, 18, 19, 20, 21, 91
Grano Illeras 18
Luis On 11, 12, 13
Eugeni Pons 20, 21
Thies Schröder 11

AGENCE TER
Alexandre Pedzol 22, 28
Agence Ter 23, 24, 25, 26, 27, 30, 31, 97

STIG L. ANDERSSON
Stig L. Andersson 33, 34, 36, 37, 38, 39, 40, 41, 103

BÜRO KIEFER
Claas Dreppenstedt 44, 45, 46, 47, 49, 50, 51
Reinhard Görner 42
Büro Kiefer 43, 48, 52, 99
Büro Kiefer und Barkow Leibinger Architekten 52
Simone Rosenberg 53

AGENCE ILEX
Agence Ilex 101
Gérard Dufresne 54, 56, 57, 58, 59, 60, 61, 62, 63

LATZ + PARTNER
Fonds de Kirchberg 66, 69
Michael Latz 73, 76, 77
Latz + Partner 65, 68, 70, 71, 75, 95
Monika Nicolic 64
Christa Panick 72, 74

MICHEL DESVIGNE / CHRISTINE DALNOKY
Desvigne & Dalnoky 78, 79, 80, 81, 82, 83, 84, 85, 86, 87, 88, 95

BET FIGUERAS
Nuria Andreu 112
Bet Figueras 93, 104, 106, 107, 108, 114
Maria Jover 115
Pepe Sancho 113
Thies Schröder 105
Oscar Tusquets 109, 110
Victoria Valenzuela 105

GUIDO HAGER
Patrick Altermatt 122, 123, 124, 125
Terence du Fresne 117, 118
Wolfgang Glutz 119
Guido Hager 96, 120
Johannes Stoffler 120

HEIKE LANGENBACH / ROMAN IVANCSICS
Hubert Dimko 126, 127
Langenbach / Ivancsics 99, 127, 128, 130, 131, 132, 133, 135, 136, 137

CORNELIA MÜLLER / JAN WEHBERG
Bitter und Bredt 143, 144, 145, 147
Stefan Müller 142
Müller / Wehberg 92, 138, 140, 143, 147, 151
Felix Nußbaum Museum Osnabrück 147
Erik-Jan Ouwerkerk 138, 141, 148, 149, 150, 151
Jürgen Wilhelm 139

ROTZLER KREBS PARTNER
Pascal Böni 155
Heinrich Helfenstein 157, 158
Peter Petschek 161
Stefan Rotzler 153, 160
Rotzler Krebs Partner 100, 158
Anton Schnyder 155, 156
Gaston Wicky 154, 159

GROSS. MAX.
Allan Dimmick 164
John MacGregor 167
GROSS. MAX. 102, 163, 165, 166, 167, 168, 169, 170
GROSS. MAX. / Mark Dion 171
Keith Hunter 163, 164, 165

WEST 8
Sabine Müller 181
Jeroen Musch 172, 173, 174, 175, 176, 177, 178, 179, 180
West 8 100, 173